DAVID MAMET

Oleanna

with commentary and notes by
DANIEL ROSENTHAL

Bloomsbury Methuen Drama
An imprint of Bloomsbury Publishing Plc

B L O O M S B U R Y
LONDON · OXFORD · NEW YORK · NEW DELHI · SYDNEY

Bloomsbury Methuen Drama
An imprint of Bloomsbury Publishing Plc

Imprint previously known as Methuen Drama

50 Bedford Square	1385 Broadway
London	New York
WC1B 3DP	NY 10018
UK	USA

www.bloomsbury.com

BLOOMSBURY, METHUEN DRAMA and the Diana logo are trademarks of Bloomsbury Publishing Plc

Oleanna first published in the United Kingdom in 1993 by Methuen Drama
This edition first published in the United Kingdom in 2004 by Methuen Publishing Ltd
Reissued with additional material and a new cover design in 2006
Reissued with a new cover design in 2009
Reprinted 2011, 2013, 2015, 2016

© David Mamet 1992
Commentary and notes © Daniel Rosenthal 2004, 2006
Chronology © Karen C. Blansfield 2004

British Library Cataloguing-in-Publication Data
A catalogue record for this book is available from the British Library.

ISBN: PB: 978-0-4137-7376-0

Library of Congress Cataloging-in-Publication Data
A catalog record for this book is available from the Library of Congress.

Series: Student Editions

Typeset by Deltatype Ltd, Birkenhead, Merseyside
Printed and bound in Great Britain

Contents

David Mamet   v

Plot   xiv

Commentary   xvii
  Mamet's themes   xvii
  Sexual and campus politics   xx
  Oleanna as tragedy   xxviii
  Structure   xxxi
  Language   xxxv
  Carol   xliv
  John   li
  Other characters   lviii
  Oleanna in performance   lxi
  Oleanna on film   lxix

Further Reading   lxxv

OLEANNA   I

Notes   81

Questions for Further Study   84

Daniel Rosenthal would like to thank David Suchet, Lia Williams and Georgina Allen for their invaluable assistance in the preparation of this edition.

David Mamet: 1947–

1947 David Alan Mamet is born on 30 November in Chicago. His father, Bernard, is a labour lawyer, and his mother, Lenora, is a teacher.

1957 Mamet's parents separate and later divorce. Mamet lives with his mother and his younger sister, Lynn, in the South Shore area of Chicago and later in the Olympia Fields suburb. The pain of his parents' divorce is, in the view of some critics, reflected in much of his work, dealing with conflicts between men and women and difficulties in male/female relationships.

1963 –5 Mamet works as a waiter at Chicago's Second City and also backstage at the Hull House Theatre. Productions staged there include works by Harold Pinter, Brecht, and Edward Albee, all of whom will prove influential in his own work. He lives with his father in Chicago's Lincoln Park area, where he attends the Francis Parker Private School.

1965 –9 Mamet attends Goddard College in Plainfield, Vermont, where he earns a BA in English Literature. He studies acting with Sanford Meisner at the Neighborhood Theatre in New York. Jobs include working as a dancer with Maurice Chevalier's Montreal company, performing in *Toutes voiles dehours!!!* at the Autostade at Montreal's 1967 Expo, and working on a cargo boat on Lake Michigan. He completes early drafts of *Sexual Perversity in Chicago*, *Duck Variations*, and *Reunion*, and for his senior thesis, he writes *Camel*, a Second City-style revue.

1969 Mamet joins a theatre company at McGill University in Toronto, where he performs in Pinter's *The Homecoming*, serves as stage manger for the long-running off-Broadway hit, *The Fantasticks*, and works in a variety of other theatre jobs. He works as office manager in a Chicago real estate office.

1970 He accepts a position as Acting instructor at Marlboro
College, Vermont, where his play *Lakeboat* is first
produced, directed by himself.

1971 He returns to Goddard College, as artist-in-residence and
to teach acting. He forms the St Nicholas Theatre
Company with two of his students. The company
performs the first versions of *Duck Variations* and *Sexual
Perversity in Chicago*, as well as a humorous piece based
on Indian legends, *Lone Canoe*.

1972 The St Nicholas Theatre Company produces *Duck
Variations* and *Sexual Perversity in Chicago* at a small
theatre in Boston. Mamet returns to Chicago, where
Duck Variations and the monologue *Litko* are performed
as a double-bill at the Body Politic Theatre.

1973 Mamet plays a minor role in a production of *The Night
They Shot Harry Lindsey With a 155mm Howitzer and
Blamed it on Zebras*, produced by the Body Politic
Theatre. He also works with a children's theatre
company, which may have inspired some of his later
writings for children.

1974 In June, *Sexual Perversity in Chicago* is presented by the
Organic Theater Company at Chicago's Leo Lerner
Theater, directed by Stuart Gordon. Mamet is artistic
director of the St Nicholas Theatre Company, which
presents *Squirrels* and *Mackinac* – a children's play – at
the Bernard Horwich Jewish Community Center in the
fall. *Sexual Perversity in Chicago* wins the Jefferson
Award for Best New Chicago Play. Mamet serves as
faculty member for the Illinois Arts Council. Gregory
Mosher is appointed as assistant to the artistic director of
the Goodman Theatre. He will become a close
collaborator with Mamet over the years, directing many
of his plays.

1975 *American Buffalo* premières at the Goodman Theatre's
Stage Two, directed by Gregory Mosher and starring
William H. Macy. In November, the St Nicholas
Company produces Mamet's *Marranos*, a play about
Jewish persecution during the Spanish Inquisition, at the
Bernard Horwich Center. The theme of Jewish identity

will pervade much of Mamet's oeuvre, including his fiction and non-fiction. *Sexual Perversity in Chicago* opens at the off-off-Broadway St Clement's Theatre, in a double bill with *Duck Variations*. *Sexual Perversity* wins the Obie Award for Best New Play. St Nicholas moves into a permanent theatre space on Halstead Street, opening with *American Buffalo*. Mamet is visiting lecturer at the University of Chicago, and contributing editor for *Oui* magazine. He gives Meisner technique-based acting classes, which will develop into a full training programme for actors as well as designers, directors, and stage managers. He writes *Revenge of the Space Pandas* for New York's St Clement's Theatre.

1976 St Nicholas Theatre produces *Squirrels* and *Reunion*. In January, *American Buffalo* opens at St Clement's Theatre, winning an Obie Award as well as a Jefferson Award for its Chicago run. Mamet resigns as artistic director of the St Nicholas Company and moves to New York. *Sexual Perversity in Chicago* and *Duck Variations* open at off-Broadway's Cherry Lane Theatre. Mamet receives a New York State Council of the Arts Grant, a Rockefeller Award and a CBS Fellowship in Creative Writing, which includes part-time teaching at Yale University.

1977 *American Buffalo* opens on Broadway in February, winning the New York Drama Critics Circle Award and later enjoying another successful run at New York's Théâtre de Lys. It marks an important development in Mamet's career, with many critics recognising a vital and unique new voice in the theatre. Goodman's Stage Two Theatre presents *A Life in the Theatre*, with Joe Mantegna, who will become another member of Mamet's regular circle. Mamet directs *All Men Are Whores* at the Yale Cabaret. In May, St Nicholas stages the première of *The Water Engine* and later the première of *The Woods*, which Mamet directs. Yale Repertory Theatre produces a double bill of *Reunion* and *Dark Pony*. *The Revenge of the Space Pandas or Binky Rudich* and *The Two-Speed Clock* are produced by the Nicholas Children's Theatre as well as in York, at Queen's Flushing Town Hall. *Duck*

Variations and *Sexual Perversity in Chicago* are produced at the Regent Theatre, London, the first European productions of Mamet's work, and run for six weeks. In December, Mamet marries actress Lindsay Crouse, who appears in many of his stage and film works.

1978 In January, *The Water Engine* is produced by Joseph Papp at the New York Shakespeare Festival Public Theater, transferring to Broadway, in a double bill at the Plymouth Theatre with *Mr Happiness*. Gregory Mosher, now artistic director of the Goodman Theatre, appoints Mamet as associate artistic director and writer-in-residence. *American Buffalo* is produced in June at London's National Theatre. *Prairie du Chien* is broadcast on BBC Radio as well as National Public Radio, which also hosts *The Water Engine*. Mamet wins the John Gassner Award for Distinguished Playwriting.

1979 Joseph Papp's Public Theater produces *The Blue Hour: City Sketches*, directed by Mamet, as well as *The Woods*. Chicago's Goodman Theatre premières *Lone Canoe, or the Explorer*, which is poorly received. More successful is a double bill of *Sexual Perversity in Chicago* and *A Sermon* at Chicago's newly opened Apollo Theater. *The Poet and the Rent* is produced at New York's Circle in the Square Repertory Theatre. PBS Television broadcasts *A Life in the Theatre*. *A Life in the Theatre* premières in London at the Open Space Theatre. In October, Mamet directs a triple bill at New York's Circle in the Square: *Reunion, Dark Pony*, and *The Sanctity of Marriage*. In December, New York's Ensemble Studio Theatre presents a short sketch, *Shoeshine*.

1980 Milwaukee Repertory Theater presents a revised version of *Lakeboat*. In New Haven, the Long Wharf Theatre stages a revival of *American Buffalo*, with Al Pacino. Mamet directs *Twelfth Night* at the Yale Repertory Theatre.

1981 Mamet's first screenplay is produced, an adaptation of James M. Cain's novel *The Postman Always Rings Twice*, directed by Bob Rafelson. He begins work on another film script, *The Verdict*. *Dark Pony* and *Reunion* are

staged in London. *American Buffalo* transfers from the
Long Wharf to Circle in the Square off-Broadway.

1982 *Lakeboat* is staged at New Haven's Long Wharf Theatre
as well as Chicago's Goodman Theatre. *Edmond*
premières at the Goodman Theatre and opens in New
York, where it wins the Obie Award. *The Verdict* is
released in December, and Mamet is nominated for an
Academy Award for Best Adapted Screenplay.

1983 In September, the world première of *Glengarry Glen Ross*
takes place at the National Theatre in London, winning
the prestigious Society of West End Theatres Award
(SWET) for Best New Play, as well as the Olivier Award.
The Goodman Theatre stages Mamet's adaptation of *Red
River* by Pierre Laville. Goodman Studio produces a triple
bill, including Mamet's *The Disappearance of the Jews*.
The New York Ensemble Theatre's Marathon Festival of
One-Act Plays presents five of Mamet's sketches as *Five
Unrelated Pieces*. *Three by Three*, another collection of
sketches, is presented in July at New York's Park Royal
Hotel and includes Mamet's *The Dog*. *American Buffalo*,
with Al Pacino and J. J. Johnston, moves to Broadway.
Mamet publishes a children's play, *The Frog Prince*.

1984 In February, the Goodman Theatre stages the American
première of *Glengarry Glen Ross*. In March it transfers
to Broadway, running for 378 performances and winning
the Pulitzer Prize, the Drama Critics Award for Best
American Play, a Joseph Dintenfass Award, and four
Tony nominations, including Best Play and Best Director
for Gregory Mosher. *American Buffalo* opens at the Duke
of York's Theatre, London. *The Frog Prince* opens at
Milwaukee Repertory Theater, and the Ensemble Studio
Theatre features *Vermont Sketches* as part of its second
Marathon Festival of One Act Plays. Mosher and Mamet
create the New Theatre Company (NTC), an independent
company featuring many of Mamet's regular associates.

1985 The New Theatre Company premières its season with
Mamet's adaptation of *The Cherry Orchard* at the
Goodman Studio. NTC later moves to a new venue, the
Briar Street Theatre, where it produces *The Shawl* and a

one-act play, *The Spanish Prisoner*, which will evolve into a major motion picture. In March, Chicago radio station WNU of Northwestern University broadcasts *Goldberg Street* and *Cross Patch*, featuring NTC members. British television's *South Bank Show* produces a programme on Mamet. Gregory Mosher is named artistic director of New York's Lincoln Center, and his first production is a double bill of *Prairie du Chien* and *The Shawl*. The film *About Last Night*, loosely based on *Sexual Perversity in Chicago*, is released. *Edmond* receives its European première at the Newcastle Playhouse, co-produced by the Royal Court Theatre, to which it transfers in December. Mamet writes *Vint* for the American Repertory Company's touring production of *Orchards*, a collection of sketches by contemporary playwrights based on Chekhov's short stories. Mamet and Macy found the Atlantic Theater Company in New York. Mamet publishes *A Collection of Dramatic Sketches and Monologues*.

1986 Mamet wins Academy Institute Award in Literature. *Prairie du Chien* and *The Shawl* are staged at the Royal Court Theatre Upstairs. *Writing in Restaurants*, a collection of Mamet's essays, is published.

1987 Mamet writes screenplay for *The Untouchables*. Also writes and directs *House of Games* – his first film as writer and director – which wins a Golden Globe Nomination for Best Screenplay. Mamet writes an episode for the TV show *Hill Street Blues*.

1988 American Repertory Theatre stages Mamet's adaptation of *Uncle Vanya*, featuring the NTC members. *Speed-the-Plow* opens at the Royale Theatre on Broadway. With Shel Silverstein, Mamet undertakes his second film as writer-director, *Things Change*, which opens the London Film Festival. Mamet's sketch *Where Were You When It Went Down?* is part of an off-Broadway revue, *Urban Blight*, directed by John Tillinger. Mamet directs *Sketches of War* at Boston's Colonial Theatre, a programme that includes Mamet's *Cross Patch*. For *The Untouchables*, Mamet earns a Writers Guild Award Nomination for Best Screenplay Based on Material from Another Medium. His children's book, *Warm and Cold*, is published.

1989 In January, *Speed-the-Plow* opens at London's National Theatre. That summer, a work-in-progress, *Bobby Gould in Hell*, receives a staged reading at the National Theatre; in December, the completed play premières at Lincoln Center's Mitzie Newhouse Theater. *The Water Engine* receives its British première at London's Hampstead Theatre Club. In October, the West End's Theatre Royal, Haymarket, stages a major revival of *A Life in the Theatre*, following a United Kingdom tour. Mamet writes another screenplay, this one for Neil Jordan's film remake, *We're No Angels*. Mamet's second collection of essays, *Some Freaks*, is published.

1990 Atlantic Theater Company performs Mamet's adaptation of Chekhov's *Three Sisters* at Philadelphia's Festival Theater. Another Mamet adaptation of Chekhov, *Uncle Vanya*, premières at the Harrogate Theatre in Britain as well as at the Goodman Theatre in the US. Mamet completes screenplays for *Hoffa*, *the Deer Slayer* (based on a James Fenimore Cooper story), *High and Low* (based on a film by Akira Kurosawa), and *Ace in the Hole*. Mamet appears on the BBC TV's *Clive James Show*. His collection of poetry, *The Hero Pony*, is published.

1991 Mamet writes and directs the film *Homicide*. His book, *On Directing Film*, is published.

1992 *Oleanna* premières at New York's American Repertory Theatre, moving to the Orpheum Theatre. Writes screenplay for *Glengarry Glen Ross*. Publishes a book of essays, *The Cabin: Reminiscence and Diversions*.

1993 British première of *Squirrels* staged at King's Head Theatre, Islington. TNT American television films *A Life in the Theatre*, with Matthew Broderick and Jack Lemmon. *Oleanna*, directed by Harold Pinter, is staged at London's Royal Court Theatre, transferring later to the Duke of York's in London's West End.

1994 Mamet writes and directs the film version of *Oleanna*, starring William H. Macy and Debra Eisenstadt. *The Cryptogram*, directed by Gregory Mosher, premières at London's Ambassadors Theatre. Sam Mendes directs a

revival of *Glengarry Glen Ross* at London's Donmar
Warehouse. *Vanya on 42nd Street*, Mamet's adaptation of
Chekhov's work, opens in New York, directed by André
Gregory. Mamet publishes three books: his novel *The
Village*, *A Whore's Profession: Notes and Essays*, and *A
Life With No Joy In It, and Other Plays and Pieces.*

1995 *The Cryptogram*, directed by Mamet, premières at
Boston's C. Walsh Theatre as well as in New York at the
Westside Theatre Upstairs. Mamet's piece *An Interview* is
included in a three-act show, *Death Defying Acts*, staged
at the Variety Arts Theatre in New York. Mamet directs
his adaptation of J.B. Priestley's *Dangerous Corner* at
New York's Atlantic Theater Company.

1996 Film version of *American Buffalo*, with screenplay by
Mamet, opens the Boston Film Festival. To celebrate its
twenty-fifth anniversary and long collaboration with
Mamet, the Ensemble Studio Theatre stages five one-acts
and monologues, including *No One Will Be Immune* and
the New York première of *Joseph Dintenfass*. Mamet
publishes another book of essays, *Make-Believe Town:
Essays and Remembrances.*

1997 *The Old Neighborhood* premières at the American
Repertory Theatre in Cambridge, Massachusetts, then
moves to Broadway at the Booth Theatre. The film *Wag
the Dog* opens, with a screenplay by Mamet and Hilary
Henkin, and is nominated for a Golden Globe Award for
Best Motion Picture, Best Screenplay, and Best Actor. It
also receives an Academy Award nomination for Best
Adapted Screenplay as well as a nomination for Best
Screenplay by the Writers Guild of America. Mamet
writes and directs *The Spanish Prisoner*, which opens the
Toronto Film Festival. Writes an original screenplay, *The
Bookworm*, which is produced as the film *The Edge.*
Publishes a book on acting, *True and False: Heresy and
Common Sense for the Actor*; *Three Uses of the Knife:
On the Nature and Purpose of Drama*, essays originally
delivered as the Columbia Lectures on American Culture;
also a historical novel, *The Old Religion.*

1998 Two Mamet plays receive their British premières: *Lakeboat* at London's Lyric Studio, Hammersmith, and *The Old Neighborhood* at the Royal Court at St Martin's Lane. *Jade Mountain* opens at the New York Ensemble Theatre's Marathon of One-Acts. Mamet's screenplay for *Ronin* is directed by John Frankenheimer. Mamet directs his film adaptation of Terence Rattigan's play, *The Winslow Boy*. He co-produces his screenplay *Lansky*, which is broadcast on HBO Television.

1999 Mamet directs the première of his *Boston Marriage* at the American Repertory Theatre. Writes screenplay for *The Cincinnati Kid*. Publishes *Jafsie and John Henry: Essays on Hollywood, Bad Boys and Six Hours of Perfect Poker*; a work of fiction, *Bar Mitzvah* and *The Chinaman*.

2000 The Donmar Warehouse, London, stages a revival of *American Buffalo* by the Atlantic Theater Company. In September, Mamet's film of Samuel Beckett's *Catastrophe* premières at the Toronto International Film Festival, featuring Harold Pinter as well as John Gielgud in his final film performance. *State and Main*, a film written and directed by Mamet, opens in December; among the honours it receives are the National Board of Review 2000 Best Ensemble Performance award as well as a nomination for Best Screenplay.

2001 The British première of *Boston Marriage* is staged at the Donmar Warehouse, London, directed by Phyllida Lloyd. *State and Main* is nominated for the Chicago Film Critics Award. *Heist*, the eighth film written and directed by Mamet, premières at the Venice Film Festival in August. *Speed-the-Plow* is staged at the Edinburgh Festival. A film version of *Lakeboat*, directed by Joe Mantegna, is released for limited general distribution. Mamet's futuristic novel *Wilson: A Consideration of the Sources*, is published. The film *Hannibal*, with screenplay by Mamet and Steven Zaillian and directed by Ridley Scott, is released.

2002 Mamet publishes *South of the Northeast Kingdom*, a collection of essays.

Plot

Act One

A university in the United States in the early 1990s. The office of John, a middle-aged professor of education. Watched by Carol, one of his first-year students, John has a fraught phone conversation with his wife, Grace, which suggests that the couple may not be able to complete the imminent purchase of their new house. John urges Grace to call their lawyer, Jerry, and promises to join her as soon as possible.

John has called Carol in to discuss the poor quality of her work. She protests that she has followed the course instructions to the letter, but cannot understand the language in John's book and lectures. John reassures her that she is not stupid, but reads out an extract from one of her essays which he feels is so meaningless that he may have to fail her.

John takes a call from Jerry about the house sale, then asks Carol how he might resolve the situation other than by failing her. When Carol gives examples of the phrases that she cannot grasp, John urges her not to take the course so seriously. She says that is impossible, because a degree is so important to her career prospects. She becomes increasingly distressed at her 'pathetic' stupidity. Slightly taken aback, John tries to reassure her by telling her how he was raised to think himself stupid and his reminiscence broadens into a theory of education which suggests that it's John's fault that Carol struggles to understand his lectures.

After John speaks to Grace on the phone, again promising to join her soon, it emerges that he is to be promoted to a tenured position. He tells Carol that they are no longer bound by teacher/student restrictions, that all exams are 'nonsense' and that Carol's final grade for his course will be an A, provided that she returns for more one-on-one meetings. Carol says this will be against university rules but John says the rules can be broken if their arrangement remains secret.

Carol is dumbfounded by his assertion that she is a victim of the prejudice that assumes all high-school leavers should automatically go to university and becomes desperately confused, almost hysterical about her inability to understand both the course and what he is saying. John puts his arm around her shoulder but she recoils. He persists in reassuring her. She says 'I'm bad' and is about to reveal a deep secret when John takes a call from Grace. John becomes furious at the prospect of losing the house and, speaking to Jerry, is threatening legal action against the female vendor when it emerges that the sale is proceeding smoothly and the calls have been a ruse, designed to get John to attend a surprise party in honour of his tenure announcement. This ends his and Carol's meeting.

Act Two
In a lengthy and pompous monologue, John tells Carol the story of his career. Carol has made a formal complaint against him but he's confident that the tenure committee will dismiss it, although this may not prevent him from losing the house and the deposit. He was shocked at the content of the report and had asked to meet her in the hope of settling the matter privately. Carol says he wants her to retract and refuses to discuss this.

John reads from the report, which brands him as a sexist élitist and includes other allegations relating to John's comments and actions in Act One. He dismisses the charges as 'ludicrous'.

Carol launches into a tirade against his hypocrisy and his abuse of the power he held over her and her fellow students. He argues for Carol to accept their differing perspectives. His wife telephones and he reassures her that the house sale will go through because he's resolving Carol's complaint. Carol says it's wrong to discuss the matter in private and attempts to leave. John restrains her and she cries out for help.

Act Three

Following a further complaint from Carol, the tenure committee has suspended John and he is facing dismissal. Carol tries to convince him that his actions have led him into this predicament and says she cannot recant because of her responsibility to her fellow students.

She quotes examples of his flirtatious remarks to his students, equates his behaviour with rape and accuses him of believing in nothing. He says he believes in freedom of thought. If so, argues Carol, why does he question the committee's verdict?

John admits to hating Carol. They argue over whether his touching her shoulder was devoid of sexual content. She insists that what she wants is for him to understand how his behaviour makes his students feel. He says further discussion is pointless because his career is finished. As she is about to leave she says her group will not proceed with its complaints if he agrees to support the withdrawal from university reading lists of several questionable books, including his own. Furious, he tells her to leave. She stays, adding that John must also sign a statement prepared by the group. He refuses to agree to either demand.

He learns in a phone call from Jerry that Carol's group may pursue criminal charges against him for battery and attempted rape. John again asks her to leave, then takes a call from Grace. Exiting, Carol tells John not to call his wife 'baby'. Enraged, he beats her, knocking her to the floor. As he is about to bring down a raised chair on her, his rage subsides and he returns to his desk.

Commentary

Mamet's themes

David Mamet has been one of the most prolific and unpredictable playwrights of the last twenty-five years. His work has introduced us to an unforgettable collection of Americans: the swinging singles of 1970s Chicago, small-time crooks, Florida real estate agents, Hollywood executives, the crew of a lakeboat. Yet while he could never be accused of repeating settings or characters, Mamet's work does contain recurrent and consistent themes, several of which are addressed in *Oleanna*.

Mamet's dramas constantly highlight the gap between the ideals of the American dream and its often shabby or cynical reality. Whatever their social or professional context, his characters seem entitled not to 'life, liberty and the pursuit of happiness' but strife, compromise and the selfish pursuit of money, sex and power. Long before Oliver Stone's film *Wall Street* (1986) introduced the phrase, many of Mamet's characters had convinced themselves that 'greed is good'.

In his real estate drama *Glengarry Glen Ross* (1983), unsuspecting clients' hopes of buying a dream home mean nothing to the shameless agents who will use whatever means necessary to close a deal. Bobby Gould, the Hollywood studio executive in *Speed-the-Plow* (1988) could choose to produce a profound film drama about the nature of human existence but opts instead for a mindless, macho prison drama. Danny and Deborah in *Sexual Perversity in Chicago* (1974) take promising first steps towards an enduring relationship until Danny's indoctrinated obsession with casual sex, and corresponding fear of love, send him sprinting from commitment.

In *Oleanna*, Carol is desperate to complete a university education that will deliver 'economic betterment', never mind if it will make her a better or more fulfilled person, while John is part of an academic system that 'hazes' its students, and he appears consistently to have put his own best interests above those of his students.

When Moss, the most abrasive of the *Glengarry* estate agents, questions the office status quo and notes angrily that 'it doesn't have to be this way', he could just as well be talking about higher education, Hollywood or heterosexual relationships.

So why are things as they are in Mamet's plays? In large part because the intrinsic, indefinable value of human activity – the various satisfactions to be drawn from work and intimate relationships – is too often swamped by the drive to win at all costs. Quantity appears to outweigh quality every time.

John has been encouraged to judge teaching success according to the size and comfort of his house and the scale of his son's private school fees, not whether he has helped Carol and her fellow students to learn. The *Glengarry* realtors must reach the top of the company's sales board to win a $6,000 bonus and a Cadillac, or risk dismissal (and one of them resorts to theft when his semi-legitimate tactics fail).

Bobby Gould faces the same threat as Moss and Co., telling his temporary secretary, Karen: 'Is there such a thing as a good film which loses money? In general, of course. But, really, not. For *me*, 'cause if the films I make lose money, then I'm back on the streets with a sweet and silly smile on my face' (*Mamet Plays: 3*, p. 152).

The small-time crooks of *American Buffalo* (1975), as Matthew C. Roudane notes in his book *American Drama Since 1960*, have such a warped view of the free enterprise culture underpinning American life that one of them, Teach, believes men are free 'to Embark on Any Fucking Course that he sees fit . . . In order to secure his honest chance to make a profit' (*Mamet Plays: 1*, p. 221).

In *Sexual Perversity*, dames count more than dollars, and Danny has succumbed to his misogynist friend Bernard's view that the more women you fuck the better and bigger man you become; love, marriage and family are for suckers.

All too often, sex becomes or is viewed as just another commodity, creating a climate in which the tenure committee in *Oleanna* can readily accept Carol's accusation that John has asked her to sleep with him in return for a higher grade. The ambitious Karen in *Speed-the-Plow* comes across as the kind of woman who would have regarded such an unscrupulous offer from a professor as fair trade, and she sleeps with Gould because she believes doing so will advance her career in Hollywood. She does not know that Gould's colleague, Charlie Fox, has bet him $500 to see if he can seduce her; both sides have an equally mercenary attitude to sex. In *Edmond*, the heterosexual transaction is at least unashamedly explicit, as we see the hero haggling tragi-comically with a prostitute over the cost of her services.

One has to look very hard to find male Mamet characters who do not disappoint, abandon or betray the women who depend on or love them – provided, that is, they have first managed to develop beyond the view expressed by both *Sexual Perversity*'s Bernard and by Fred, one of the sailors in the all-male world of *Lakeboat* (1980): 'The Way to Get Laid is to Treat 'Em Like Shit' (*Mamet Plays: 1*, p. 58, and *Plays: 2*, p. 206).

In *Oleanna*, John fails Carol as a teacher and his arrogant insensitivity towards her jeopardises his apparently successful marriage to Grace. Danny misguidedly treats Deborah as just another lay in *Sexual Perversity*. In the opening scene of *Edmond* the hero leaves the wife who has not interested him 'spiritually or sexually' for years; in *The Cryptogram* the unseen husband, Robert, leaves his wife, Donny, and young son for his mistress and, to compound Donny's misery, it turns out that Del, Robert's best friend, has known about and aided the affair. When Donny says 'If I could find *one man*. In my life. Who would not betray me . . .' she might be speaking not just about Del and Robert, but any number of Mamet men. The hard-won devotion between Jolly and her husband, Carl, in *Jolly*, the second of the three short plays in *The Old Neighborhood* (1997), is all the more touching because it is so rare within Mamet's oeuvre.

Matthew Roudane writes: 'Mamet often concerns himself with the near-complete separation of the individual from genuine relationship' (*American Drama Since 1960*, p. 161). This isolation is most powerfully and consistently defined through the characters' failure to communicate; Carol and John are far from the only Mamet characters for whom 'Do you see?' and 'I don't understand' are almost catchphrases.

Words are of little use in bridging the gulfs between the characters, and audiences who listen to Carol and John, the crooks of *American Buffalo* or Gould and Fox in *Speed-the-Plow* hear individuals pursuing their own agenda, hidden or otherwise, or just saying something, *anything*, either to pass the time or to avoid saying how they feel about themselves, their lives or each other.

Sexual and campus politics

More than any other of Mamet's plays, *Oleanna* was written as a direct response to contemporary events in the United States. In the late 1980s and early 1990s, the rise of the political correctness (PC) movement on campuses and a series of high-profile lawsuits in which women accused male colleagues of sexual harassment in the workplace had become major issues and Mamet quickly identified their theatrical potential.

When American theatregoers first encountered *Oleanna*, therefore, they saw in the conflict between Carol and John a battle very much like the ones they had already seen unfold in newspaper reports or on the TV news. This was dramatic art reacting to and imitating life with speed and fury.

Political correctness
The political correctness lobby that John denounces in the closing seconds of *Oleanna* had an immensely disruptive and divisive impact on American universities in the late 1980s and early 1990s.

In 1992, the year of *Oleanna*'s American première, a collection of essays was published, *Debating PC – The Controversy over Political Correctness on College Campuses*. Its blurb identified the PC debate as 'the most important discussion in American education today ... [which] has grown into a major national controversy raging on the covers of our top magazines and news shows.'

The PC movement originated on the left wing of American campus politics and was, in broadly defined terms, a reaction against the perceived dominance of university governance and course content (predominantly in humanities faculties) by a white, male, middle-class élite – the élite represented in the play by John and opposed by the female, lower-class Carol.

This élite was attacked for supporting a curriculum described as follows in *Debating PC*, in an essay by Paula Rothenberg, professor of philosophy and women's studies at the William Paterson College of New Jersey: 'The traditional curriculum teaches all of us to see the world through the eyes of privileged, white, European males and to adopt their interests and perspectives as our own.' This curriculum, she adds, 'teaches all of us to use white male values and culture as the standard by which everyone and everything else is to be measured and found wanting' (p. 265). They were, in short, subjected to the accusations levelled against John by Carol.

The academic establishment counter-attacked with as much force as it could muster, chiefly through the professors' organisation, the National Association of Scholars. They denounced the vindictive climate in which experienced teachers were being obliged to move to different departments just to carry on with the work they'd been doing for years.

The conflict became so intense that even Republican President George Bush Snr, who as *Debating PC* editor Paul Berman wrote, was 'not otherwise known as a university intellectual or a [free speech] hard-liner, weighed in with a speech defending campus freedoms against "politically correct" censors'.

A number of real-life cases anticipated or echoed aspects of *Oleanna*. Carol and her group's attempt to have several books, including John's, removed from the university reading list, is far from the stuff of fantasy. Reading lists were major sources of contention on US campuses at the time, with pressure exerted by both sides of the PC debate. Minority groups campaigned for and in many cases won the right to broaden humanities set texts beyond the traditional canon of literature by 'dead white males' and non-fiction texts written by white historians, leading to the introduction of books representing newer movements such as 'hyperethnicity' and 'Afrocentrism'.

In 1990, at the University of Texas, Austin, the introduction of a new syllabus for the first-year students' compulsory English composition course included a left-wing anthology, *Racism and Sexism*, edited by Paula Rothenberg. Faculty members argued that a book with such an overtly political slant had no place on a composition course designed for all students. The policy committee which had chosen the book resigned en masse and it was dropped from the syllabus.

Carol's criticism of John's 'sexist, classist' language came at a time when several American universities had, amid great controversy, introduced 'speech codes' for staff and students. These sought to ban 'offensive' language; specifically, in the case of the University of California, derogatory references to 'race, sex, sexual orientation, or disability'. Breach of the California code was punishable by a formal reprimand or dismissal from the university.

In September 1993 Mamet told *The Times* that before he began writing *Oleanna*, a friend had told him of a young academic who made a 'loose' remark in class and was then prosecuted through the university's disciplinary system for the next two years, not by the student involved, who did not want to pursue the matter, but by one of her advisers.

Attempts to control language and debate became so severe that *Newsweek* magazine ran a cover story labelling the PC movement as a modern-day descendant of the Thought Police in Orwell's *Nineteen Eighty-Four*.

Sexual harassment

Interviewed on American television's *Charlie Rose Show*, November 1994, Mamet recalled: 'There seemed to be such vehemence surrounding the issue of sexual harassment that part of me really didn't want to raise my head up above the foxhole and say "What's going on here?"' (quoted in Kane, 2001, p. 175).

In the late 1980s, accepted codes of behaviour between men and women in America had been challenged as never before. Remarks that had previously been accepted (or perhaps, by women, tolerated) as part of everyday discourse were labelled sexist and demeaning. One man's innocent sexual flirtation was suddenly sexual harassment, in the workplace or on campus, and liable to result in some form of prosecution, whether through internal disciplinary hearings or a lawsuit.

Just as Mamet had responded to the post-sexual-revolution promiscuity of the urban American singles scene in his 1974 play *Sexual Perversity in Chicago*, he now detected another change in male-female relationships. '[America] has always been a Puritan country, and we've always been terrified of sex,' Mamet told interviewers from *Playboy* magazine in 1995. 'That terror takes different forms. Sometimes it is over-indulgence, and, of course, at other times [such as the early 1990s] it's the opposite' (ibid., p. 123).

Asked what was behind the repressive atmosphere, he pointed to the economic recession that prevented the young from envisaging financially secure futures for themselves and their putative families. 'You can't become committed to somebody because you can't support a family and recreational sex [so tempting in the 1970s and 1980s] is out because Aids might kill you. As a result, society is going to bring us to some sort of intermediary mechanism, something to keep people wary of getting involved with each other. Here it comes – sexual harassment.'

Harassment in the workplace and on campus was bound up with the other 'hot-button issue' of PC when Mamet began work on *Oleanna* in 1989–90, while he was living in Cambridge, Massachusetts, home to Harvard, America's most prestigious university. As the idea of writing about this topic developed, Mamet could draw not only on contemporary stories, but also on first-hand observations of *Oleanna*'s campus setting and central relationships, gleaned through his work teaching acting at Goddard College, Vermont, the university where he had been an undergraduate. He has recalled that when he taught at Goddard in 1971 many of the young professors were having relationships with female students.

Contrast that easygoing sexual culture with the America of the early 1990s, when the University of Virginia imposed an official ban on teacher-student relationships. A survey by America's Center for Women's Policy Studies found that one in fifty female undergraduates would be offered higher grades for sex (precisely the scenario implied in Carol's evidence to the tenure committee) and that twenty per cent of female undergraduates had been sexually harassed.

While he was living in Cambridge, Mamet 'used to hear these stories about sexual harassment. So-and-so had a brother who got fired because he said "blah, blah, blah"; or so-and-so had a niece and the professor came on to her, and she had to "blah, blah blah". So I sat down and started making up a fantasy about an interchange between a young woman who wants her grade changed and a professor who wants to get her out of the office so he can go home to see his wife, and one thing led to another, and the story kind of evolved and became this story about the power struggle between the two' (*Charlie Rose Show*, quoted in Kane, 2001, p. 163).

Clarence Thomas v. Anita Hill
In America, *Oleanna*'s topicality was massively enhanced by the 1991 case involving judge Clarence Thomas and law professor Anita Hill. Thomas was an African-American judge whose nomination to the Supreme Court by Republican President George Bush Snr was challenged by the Democrats when Hill, also African-American, alleged that Thomas had subjected her to prolonged and consistent sexual harassment when she was his assistant years earlier.

Their legal battle, in which Hill's reputation was savaged and Thomas's place on the Supreme Court was eventually ratified, was televised and became a forerunner to the Bill Clinton/Monica Lewinsky scandal, with media and public picking over every salacious detail.

Hours of airtime and acres of newsprint were devoted to arguments over what the case said about sexual politics in 1990s America and when *Oleanna* opened, many American theatre critics referred to John and Carol as Mamet's Clarence Thomas and Anita Hill. Frank Rich, in the *New York Times*, called it 'an impassioned response to the Thomas hearings . . . [which] leaves us feeling much the same way as the hearings did: soiled and furious'.

In fact, Mamet had been more prescient than opportunistic. He told his *Playboy* interviewers that he had written the first version of the play before the Thomas/Hill hearings began, then 'stuck it in a drawer. It seemed a little farfetched to me. And then the Thomas hearings began, and I took the play out of the drawer and started working on it again. One of the first people to see the play was a headmaster at a very good school in Cambridge [Mass.]. He said to me: "Eighteen months ago I would have said this play was fantasy. But now, when all the headmasters get together at conferences, we whisper to one another, 'You know, all of us are only one dime away from the end of a career'"' (op.cit., p. 138).

These circumstances help to explain the vehemence of the audience responses to *Oleanna* that are described on p. lxv.

Student anxiety

In discussing his portrayal of Carol, Mamet has said that at the time he wrote the play, young people like her were frightened: 'They wonder why they're in college, what they're going to do when they get out, what has happened to society. Nobody's looking out for them, and there's nothing for them to go into. It's no wonder they're trying to take things into their own hands' (ibid.).

To appreciate Carol's fixation on the need 'to get on in the world' through university study, it's important to appreciate that the American university system is largely private, with parents and students paying tens of thousands of dollars a year in tuition.

Students enter this system with clearly defined expectations: if they work hard and secure a college qualification, they will get a good job and salary that will enable them to pay off their debts and have a comfortable life (hence John's reference in *Oleanna* to statistics of wage-earning for the college-educated).

In studying Carol, it's also worth noting that Mamet wrote the part for his wife, the actress Rebecca Pidgeon, whom he had met at the National Theatre, London, in 1989, when she was appearing in his Hollywood satire, *Speed-the-Plow*, as a movie producer's secretary (an apparently guileless but ultimately manipulative character well worth considering as a forerunner to *Oleanna*'s Carol, particularly because she is initially presented as timid but is revealed to be more intelligent and manipulative than her male superiors, the producers Gould and Fox, first assumed).

Other writers on PC and harassment

Mamet was not alone in seeking a fictional response to America's real-life preoccupation with sexual harassment and political correctness in the 1990s. The plot of Michael Crichton's best-selling 1994 novel *Disclosure* (turned into a Hollywood film in the same year), involves Tom Sanders, an executive in a Seattle computer company, who comes close to having sex with his ex-lover and new boss Meredith Johnson in her office. Furious at being spurned, she then accuses him of sexually harassing her. The rest of the book is devoted to the legal battle between them.

The story hinges on the same dramatic premise as *Oleanna* – a man and a woman's conflicting accounts of a private meeting, when the reader/audience knows that the woman is exaggerating or lying. A critic for the *Seattle Weekly* wrote of the film of *Oleanna*: 'David Mamet beats *Disclosure* to the sexual harassment punch' and Crichton's is a much cruder work, with cardboard characters and improbable plot twists. The film does, however, contain one memorable line which Carol would appreciate, when Tom's lawyer tells him: 'Sexual harassment isn't about sex, it's about power.'

Oleanna's concern with the impact on campus life of political correctness and the twisting of language also lies at the heart of Philip Roth's 2000 novel *The Human Stain* (turned into a Hollywood film in 2003). Its hero, Coleman Silk, is a classics professor who, one day in 1998 (the year of the Clinton/

Lewinsky scandal), notes the continued absence of two students
who have yet to attend a single class. He asks the rest of the
group: 'Do they exist or are they spooks?' He clearly intends
the word to mean 'ghosts' or 'phantoms', but the two students,
African-Americans, accuse Silk of having used the alternative
meaning of 'spook', as a racist epithet akin to 'nigger'. Silk is
so outraged at his colleagues for obliging him to defend the
accusation that he resigns, with a series of tragic consequences.

  Disgrace (1999), the Booker Prize-winning novel by the South
African writer J.M. Coetzee, provides an interesting
counterpoint to Mamet's take on campus sexual harassment.
Here a middle-aged academic is punished by a disciplinary
panel for an actual affair with a vulnerable student and (as
with *The Human Stain*), we see what might happen to a
teacher like John after his dismissal.

  Like *Disclosure* and *The Human Stain*, *Oleanna* is absolutely
a product of its times, but it will continue to enrage and move
audiences who have never heard of Clarence Thomas and Anita
Hill. As Mamet said to Charlie Rose: 'Basically what I wanted
to do . . . is just to simply tell a story. That something is an
important topic in our daily newspaper or in our breakfast-
table discussion does not necessarily mean that it's going to
make a good play' (op.cit., p. 166).

  For David Suchet, who played John in the London première,
Oleanna will endure because 'rather like Shakespeare it's
dealing with a universal theme of male-female relationships.
You could put the situation into any age and any establishment
– a business, law courts, the army – and it would still work.
That's what makes it a great play.'

A note on the title: Oleanna was a failed nineteenth-century
Utopian commune in Wisconsin, so there is an immense, ironic
gap between the title's allusion to an idyllic community in
which men and women live in harmony and the dramatisation
of an academic community riven by sexual and linguistic
tension and argument. The jaunty folk song 'Olé Anna' was
played over the public address as the lights went down for the
start of each performance in the Royal Court production,
fading out as the play began.

Oleanna as tragedy

In his introduction to *Mamet Plays: 4*, which contains *Oleanna*, Mamet describes the play as 'a classical tragedy' about power, which, like the earliest dramas of ancient Greece, uses just two actors, playing a protagonist and an antagonist. But how useful is the tragedy label in assessing *Oleanna*, and how closely does the play conform to the conventions of classical tragedy?

If we agree with Mamet that *Oleanna* is a tragedy then the tragic outcome is the destruction of John's career and comfortable home life, but Mamet makes it impossible for us definitively to apportion blame to either party, and the equivocal nature of the drama and our responses to it is neatly summed up by the publicity tag-line for the film of *Oleanna*: 'Whichever side you take, you're wrong'. As Mamet said in an interview for the *South Bank Show* television programme in 1994: 'I don't . . . personally take the side of one rather than the other. I think they're absolutely both wrong, and they're absolutely both right. And that's to the extent that the play aspires to – or achieves – the status of a tragedy.'

The text that has had the greatest influence on Western definitions of tragic drama is the *Poetics*, written by Aristotle in the fourth century BC. In it, he states that the most important component of a tragedy is the plot, which should have 'a beginning, middle and end'. The plot should 'allow the hero by a series of probable or necessary stages to pass from happiness to misfortune'. The best tragic plots, Aristotle argued, involve a man who is not exceptionally virtuous and whose downfall results from errors of judgment, not vice. There should be unity of place and action; events that advance the plot but take place elsewhere must be reported by the chorus or another character, rather than shown.

Measured by these three criteria, *Oleanna* is certainly a classical tragedy. Act One gives us the beginning, Two the middle and Three the end. John moves from happiness to misfortune and, as discussed in detail on pp. li–lvii, Mamet shows John making a series of errors of judgment that contribute to his downfall (a professor who is known to have raped one of his students in the play would not fit Aristotle's definition of tragedy, because he would be guilty of depravity).

We have unity of place, as all three acts are set in John's office, and unity of action because the events that advance the plot (Carol's meetings with her group; the tenure committee hearings, etc.) are reported by John, Carol or the telephone, which, says Mamet 'functions, as per usual, as a chorus or title card – to introduce new information, emotional or factual, or to comment upon the old'. Without the telephone the plot could only be advanced by scenes set in other locations.

The chorus/telephone also enables Mamet to use a staple shock effect in tragic drama, whereby the hero and audience are allowed to think that he has reached the lowest point in his misfortune, only to be brought news of a still greater calamity. In *King Lear*, for example, we see the king driven mad, defeated in battle, *then* bring on the corpse of his daughter, Cordelia, hanged.

In *Oleanna*, we think that John's dismissal and the loss of his new home are his most severe punishments, only for the final phone call from Jerry to reveal that he may face criminal prosecution, followed by the actual assault. Both plots subscribe to the belief expressed by Edgar in *King Lear* that for protagonists and audience in dramatic tragedy: 'the worst is not/So long as we can say "This is the worst".'

In the *Poetics*, Aristotle said that the hero's journey should arouse pity and fear in the audience, allowing them to be purged of these emotions by *catharsis* (meaning a purification). In his introduction to *Mamet Plays: 4*, Mamet writes: 'In the hubristic, blind, or otherwise self-absorbed gropings of the hero towards his goal (that is to say, his destruction), we see our own human state: supposedly free to act, but each elaboration of freedom-of-choice bringing us closer to the realisation that we are bound. We are bound by our character, by our lack of self-knowledge, by the inscrutable ways of gods. To recognise this, and to avow it, is to lay our burden down, to surrender – which is the meaning of *catharsis*.'

It is this self-recognition that, Mamet continues, made audience members at *Oleanna* 'scream at the actors, fight with each other after and even during the play ... The play moved the audience out of itself.' The extremes of audience reaction are discussed at greater length on pp. lxv–lxvii.

In Greek tragedy, the hubris to which Mamet refers above was defined as an insolence or arrogance towards a higher power – invariably the gods – that invites calamity. In this respect *Oleanna* may be compared to Euripides' *Bacchae*, another tragedy that dramatises a destructive conflict between diametrically-opposed viewpoints. Euripides' hero, Pentheus, is a man of power who stands for reason and self-control in human behaviour and is guilty of hubris for openly defying the god Dionysus, who wishes men and women to abandon themselves to sensual pleasure. Pentheus' punishment for this defiance is to be torn limb from limb by Dionysus' followers, the Bacchae.

In *Oleanna*, Euripides' tragic conflict between the leader of a repressive regime, Pentheus, and a libertarian revolutionary, Dionysus, is transposed to an American campus, with the politics of the leading roles reversed. In Mamet's play, the forces of revolution, Carol and her group, are the repressors, while the authority figure, John, stands for tolerance. It is not unreasonable to view John as a modern-day Pentheus: a powerful figure who defends freedom of language and expression against Carol and her group, who seek to impose uniform standards of behaviour on all men and women.

John's hubris is his defiance of the higher (but still earthly) power that exists in the world of the play: the tenure committee who take Carol's side. It is expressed repeatedly, for example in his assertion in Act Two that 'They will dismiss your complaint', and his confidence in Act Three that he can persuade Carol to withdraw her complaint, when he still talks of allegations even after he has been found guilty. John's hubris is duly punished and, although the comparison with Pentheus should not be stretched too far, Mamet's hero sees his career and home life (though not his body) torn apart by his own actions and a fanatical group.

Mamet himself has compared John to Oedipus, king of Thebes, who in Sophocles' *Oedipus the King*, learns that the plague which has befallen his kingdom has been caused because he has unwittingly killed his father and married his own mother, Jocasta. Although he has not acted maliciously, John is gradually forced to acknowledge his responsibility for Carol's actions, and in an interview with John Lahr Mamet said of his hero: 'He undergoes absolute reversal of situation, absolute recognition at the last moment of the play. He realises that perhaps he is the cause of the plague on Thebes' (*Paris Review* 39, no. 142, Spring 1997).

Within *Oleanna*, Mamet's most explicit allusion to John's place among the roster of tragic heroes comes during John's long speech at the start of Act Two, when he reflects on his shock at reading the tenure committee's report on his behaviour: 'Then I thought: is it not always at those points at which we reckon ourselves unassailable that we are most vulnerable and . . .' (p. 45). This might almost be John speaking as a professor of dramatic literature, rather than education, commenting on tragic heroes, many of them in Shakespeare, who find to their cost that pride comes before a fall. In *Othello*, for example, by the middle of the play Othello has won Desdemona as his wife and defeated the Turks in battle – like John at the end of Act One he is triumphant in his personal and professional lives – and it is in this apparently secure position that he is most vulnerable to Iago's malice, and the scheme that will fatally exploit his errant judgment. At the climax of *Macbeth*, even as his last few loyal officers fly to his enemies, Macbeth may confidently declare 'I cannot taint with fear', still believing the witches' guarantee of his invincibility; yet he is minutes away from destruction.

Othello and *Macbeth* both end with their hero's violent death – the definitive full stop to a tragic narrative. Mamet denies his audience the potentially comforting finality that allows us to say of the hero: 'He has suffered and caused others to suffer, but at least his suffering is over.' We leave *Oleanna* disturbed by what we have witnessed and wonder what will happen to John and Carol in the unwritten scenes and years to come.

Structure

Although each one of Carol's and John's meetings is self-contained and takes place on a different day, *Oleanna*'s structure is anything but episodic. Though there are only two significant incidents – John's restraint of Carol and the climactic assault – the play has a tightly-woven plot with the

beginning, middle and end stipulated by Aristotle in his *Poetics*.
Everything that John says and does in Act One has a bearing
on the characters' argument in Act Two (which is why few
plays depend so heavily on an audience paying close attention
to every line) and the second act operates both as a
development of the arguments and, in cinematic terms, as a
sustained flashback to what we have seen and heard in Act
One. Mamet is almost conjuring a split-screen effect, by which
the audience watches John and Carol dissecting the former's
behaviour in Act One, while also replaying in its 'mind's eye'
what was actually said.
So when, for example, John quotes from Carol's report to
the tenure committee:

> 'Told a rambling, sexually explicit story, in which the frequency
> and attitudes of fornication of the poor and rich are, it would
> seem, the central point ... moved to *embrace* said student.'
> (p. 47)

we think back to John's apparently inconsequential recollection
of 'some jerk thing' told him by a schoolmate that meant
'nothing', and to the physical contact between them (see p. lxiv
for the original London cast's approach to this), and we must
judge retrospectively whether John was embracing or
comforting. The dialogue in Act Two is, as it were, laid over
our and the characters' memories and interpretations of Act
One.
Act Three is constructed along similar lines, but the flashback
effect is extended to take in not only their contradictory views
of the vital incident that we have just seen:

> CAROL: To lay a hand on someone's shoulder.
> JOHN: It was devoid of sexual content.
> CAROL: I say it was not. I SAY IT WAS NOT. (p. 70)

but also ongoing arguments about John's behaviour in Act One
and earlier remarks which pre-date the start of the play:

> CAROL: (*She reads from her notes*)
>   The twelfth: 'Have a good day, dear.'
>   The fifteenth: 'Now, don't *you* look fetching ...' (p. 66)

If the whole play can be viewed as John's trial, then Act One is his case for the defence, Two is Carol's prosecution and cross-examination, Act Three is her summing-up.

Mamet's construction also involves several 'mirror' effects that reflect the shift in power through the course of the play. He uses a subtle form of repetition with variation and escalation – moments in Act Two echo and intensify their equivalents in Act One and moments in Act Three do the same for their equivalents in both previous scenes.

Three times John tells Grace that everything is going to turn out fine, but the only time he's right is in Act One, when the threat to their stability is the one she has invented to keep the surprise party a secret. At the start of Act One:

> We *aren't* going to lose the deposit. All right? I'm sure it's going to be . . .' [the audience automatically adds in his unspoken 'all right'.] (p. 2)

Near the end of Act Two, John tells Grace that they are not going to lose the house:

> because the deal is going to go *through* . . . because I know . . . be . . . will you please? Just *trust* me. Be . . . well, I'm dealing with the complaint. (p. 55)

Finally, at the end of Act Three, when Grace has just learned from Jerry of the attempted rape charge against her husband, John insists: 'No, no, it's going to be all right.' (p. 79).

This sets off a powerful echo in our minds, because the gaps between these ostensibly identical promises indicate how far John has slipped from the lofty position he occupied at the start. The first promise was confidently made in response to what turned out to be an imaginary threat; the second is made when the threat is real and his position is vulnerable but he still believes that the tenure committee will exonerate him; the third is made when it's clear that he has no way out of a genuine and much more severe situation.

The triplicate structure is reinforced because all three acts end with John pushed into behaviour that is (or can be interpreted as) aggressive, on a convincingly escalating scale.

In Act One, when Carol has yet to emerge as John's

antagonist, Mamet provides him with another enemy: the female vendor who appears to be jeopardising the purchase of his family's new home. When John thinks that the various negotiating tactics he has recommended in the earlier phone calls have come to nothing, the vendor provokes our first glimpse of an aggressive streak, albeit in language rather than action, as John tells Jerry:

> *Listen, screw* her. You *tell* her ... [...] Leave her there, leave her to *stew* in it ... [...] I'll be damned if I'll sit in the same rrr ... the next, you tell her the next time I *see* her is in court. (p. 39)

The threat swiftly turns out to have been redundant, but the aggression is real and, hearing this, we wonder – and so, surely, does Carol – how John would behave if he were standing face to face with this woman. An answer arrives at the end of Act Two.

Here, when the supremely confident John of Act One has been pushed on to the defensive by Carol's accusations and when rational argument has failed to remove the now genuine threat to his new home, he resorts to the physical action – '(*He restrains her from leaving.*)' – that, however forcefully or gently it is played on stage, Carol will interpret as attempted rape. When language fails, physical aggression is the last resort.

This escalation reaches its climax at the end of Act Three, when the same pattern is repeated: John has initiated a meeting, John tries and fails to convince Carol to do what he wants, John resorts to verbal/physical aggression, this time an actual assault.

In each act, the content of a document written or co-written by Carol, and John's response to it, are crucial indicators of the balance of power. First comes Carol's essay, written on John's instruction and of whose merit he is the absolute judge; he can humiliate her by reading out an extract and dismissing it by asking: 'What can that mean?'

In Act Two, we have Carol's report to the tenure committee, written not to order but prompted by her own anger and, we presume, after encouragement from her group. Even though the committee are to judge this document's worth, John treats it precisely as though it were another essay, reading extracts aloud and dismissing them as '*ludicrous*' – despite acknowledging that her writing will cost him his house. Carol's writing, initially passive and meaningless, becomes active and full of contentious meaning.

Finally, at the end of Act Three, she presents documents that are meant to let her and her group control John, first through the list of books they want him to condemn, then the statement that would complete their appropriation of his language and voice. She begins by writing as John's subservient pupil, becomes his accuser and judge and ends by attempting to become his blackmailing speechwriter. The documents form part of the play's dramatic spine, acting as staging posts that mark Carol's and John's status in each act.

Language

JOHN: *I'm sorry I interrupted you*
Flick through the first scene of *Oleanna*, concentrating on the shape of the lines without reading the words, and you can tell immediately that this is a play about two people failing hopelessly to communicate. Single or half-lines dominate, dozens of them ending in ellipsis because the speaker is interrupted or cannot quite find the right words to complete their initial thought, or realises that that initial thought would have been better left unspoken. Questions are answered with questions.

Form and content are inseparable: language is one of the principal subjects of the play – its use, abuse and (mis)interpretation – and the shapes and rhythms of the dialogue reflect that concern. Mamet describes *Oleanna*'s language as 'free verse'. It is imbued with a rhythmic quality that separates it from 'prose' stage dialogue that seeks to mirror everyday conversation, but is not bound to conform to strict metric rules, such as those governing the five-beat iambic pentameters of Shakespearean blank verse.

'Free verse' is a liberating form for the playwright, allowing Mamet constantly to change tempo to match the tensions between John and Carol. In musical terms, the dominant mode

of Act One is a staccato duet, compared by Lia Williams, who
played Carol in the original London production of *Oleanna*, to
'improvised jazz'. When we watch *Oleanna* in performance we
become accustomed to that dominant rhythm, to hearing two
actors' voices in fractured discord (the antithesis of, say, a
lovers' duet in Shakespeare's *Romeo and Juliet*, where the two
instruments are in synchronised harmony). As a result, the
moments when the characters play a 'solo' – most notably
John's long speech at the start of Act Two, and Carol's tirades
against him in Act Three – have a disproportionately powerful
effect on us, standing out far more than in a play whose
characters exchange speeches of more equal length and weight.

In the world of *Oleanna*, to speak uninterrupted for even
half a dozen lines is to signal that you hold the upper hand,
and if you repeat the exercise of flicking through the play,
Carol's transformation is evident in how much she says in each
scene, even before one considers what she says.

In Act One, John has perhaps eighty per cent of the dialogue
and when Carol does manage to speak for more than a couple
of lines (look in particular at the four speeches beginning 'No.
No. There are *people* out there'; 'Nobody *tells* me anything';
'No, you're right', on pp. 12 and 14, and *'Any* of it. *Any* of it'
on p. 36) she is merely describing her actions and reiterating
her low self-worth – in short, repeating at greater length what
she says elsewhere in the scene in dozens of single or half-lines.
By the end of Act One we have heard her strike the same
chords over and over again without getting through to John.

In Act Two, with Carol empowered by her report to the
tenure committee, and John's confidence somewhat shaken, the
balance of dialogue is closer to 60/40 in John's favour and
Carol's language changes in quantity and emphasis.

Look closely at her lines in Act One, and you see that most
of the verbs take the first person singular, 'I', 'me' or 'my', as
she tries in vain to explain her problems. In Act Two, look at
the preponderance of 'you's as John becomes the subject of
many of her sentences and the object of her formerly self-
directed derision.

In Act Three, the prime signal that John's fortunes have gone
into terminal decline is that he is losing his voice. Carol now

has more than half of the dialogue and she not only
appropriates his language, using it as a weapon against him,
but she begins to speak *for* him, quoting from his book, and, at
p. 64, pre-empting his lines of self-defence: 'you are going to
tell me that you have a wife and child. You are going to say
that you have a career and that you've worked for twenty
years for this.'

Her insistent 'I don't think that I need your help. I don't
think I need anything that you have' is backed up by three tiers
of linguistic evidence: quantity, direction (towards John, not
herself) and, lastly, vocabulary, through her appropriation of
John's mode of speech.

In performance, the effect on an audience is not as schematic
as this quantitative assessment might suggest. Yet, to sustain
the musical analogy, while *Oleanna* is a duet from first to last,
John's voice is the dominant instrument of Act One, the two
voices are in counterpoint in Act Two, and Carol's dominates
Act Three.

For Lia Williams, 'Carol was the hardest part I've ever had
to learn, simply because of that staccato style, the broken
sentences, and the swift thought changes and the fact that so
much of the play is just a sequence of interruptions. It was
almost impossible to learn the lines separately from David
[Suchet, who played John] because you need the cues, but once
it's in your head it plays like jazz. It's a brilliantly realised
piece of writing because thought was transferred into the
structure of each sentence in the most perfect way. You could
not leave a 'dot dot' pause where there are three dots indicated,
because it would change the way the audience interpreted it.'

Williams tells a story that illustrates how Mamet writes with
musical notation. When the script first arrived, certain words
had been underlined and in the first read-through, Suchet and
Williams found themselves 'awkwardly' emphasising those
words. 'We wondered why we were doing it and it got terribly
in the way,' Williams explains. Harold Pinter, the director,
asked Mamet for a script without the underscoring and Mamet
initially refused, saying that, musically, the emphases were
correct. 'Harold persisted,' Williams recalls, 'saying that this
script would strangle us as actors, and an unmarked script was

eventually sent.' After four weeks' rehearsal, the cast referred back to the underscored script and found that they were playing virtually every line with exactly the emphases originally indicated. 'That was just extraordinary,' says Williams.

The relationship between rhythm and meaning is vital in performance, she adds, particularly in the more fractured exchanges: 'In Mamet, as in Pinter's own plays, the punctuation is as crucial as the line and the thought behind the line. What isn't said is as important as what is said. In a sense you don't really need to understand what your character is saying, but if you play the rhythm it'll work and be coherent to an audience.'

Throughout the play, Mamet uses italics to indicate that the actor should give special emphasis to an individual word (e.g. 'I'm *smiling* in class, I'm *smiling*, the whole time. What are you *talking* about?', p. 36). But he does not specify the tone of voice as many other modern dramatists do. To take just one example: in Act One of Edward Albee's *A Delicate Balance* (1966), middle-class hostess Claire, in her late fifties, asks after the well-being of her friend Harry:

> CLAIRE (*exaggerated, but not unkind*): How's the old Harry?
> HARRY (*self-pity entering*): Pretty well, Claire, not as good as I'd like, but . . . (Pocket Books, New York, 1967, p. 48)

Thus, while emphasis in *Oleanna* may, as Williams recalls, be built into the punctuation and rhythm of the text, Mamet leaves actor and director free to find an appropriate tone in rehearsal and performance. Mamet also guides both actors towards stressing individual words by adding initial capital letters to words that do not normally require them:

> CAROL: If you would like me to speak to the Tenure Committee, here is my list. You are a Free Person, you decide. (p. 74)
> JOHN: All right. (*Pause*) I came *late* to teaching. And I found it Artificial. (p. 22)

His use of full capital letters is another indicator of special emphasis, but not necessarily a surge in volume like a composer's *fortissimo* in a musical score. Again, this leaves the actor a degree of freedom. So, for example, when Lia Williams came to:

> CAROL: NO, NO – I DON'T UNDERSTAND. DO YOU SEE???
> I DON'T UNDERSTAND . . . (p. 36)

She delivered the lines with quiet desperation; another actor might choose to yell.

JOHN: *That is not what I meant at all*

Carol's report to the tenure committee illustrates how there can be two conflicting sides to every conversation if, as the PC lobby wishes, we divorce language from its context and deny its flexibility. Superficially accurate descriptions of what we have seen John say and do in Act One are used to establish a damning pattern of behaviour.

For instance, 'he told me he had problems with his wife'. We know that John was referring principally (and perhaps exclusively) to the apparent problems with the house purchase, but the tenure committee will infer trouble in the marital bed – the kind of trouble that causes middle-aged men to make improper advances towards young female students.

Politically correct interpretation means that previously innocuous words can become poisonous; one person's inoffensive dirty joke – John's reference in Act One to the sex habits of rich and poor – becomes Carol's '*vile* and *classist*, and *manipulative* and *pornographic* story' in Act Two. Both have a valid point of view in attacking and defending the story, and Mamet has said that 'if I didn't believe them [both], the play wouldn't work as well'.

Mamet's condemnation of political correctness is implicit in the harm caused to both characters by their linguistic battle, which is why the moment when Mamet has John cry: 'You vicious little bitch. You think you can come in here *with your political correctness* and destroy my life?' [my italics] strikes one of the few false notes. *Oleanna* is too powerful a play for the audience to need the equivalent of a *Jerry Springer Show* caption ('Political Correctness Destroyed My Life!') to name and shame a doctrine as the real villain of the piece.

CAROL: *You'll have to explain that word to me*

In *Oleanna*, command of language is power. Perhaps the clearest indications of Carol's increasing assertiveness through the play are provided by her responses to individual words or phrases used by John.

In Act One, Carol is almost like an English student trying to speak a foreign language; her struggle to understand John's book and lectures appears to be more a failure of vocabulary than of intellect. She can keep up with a line of argument until, like a foreign-language student taking dictation, she hits the brick wall represented by a noun or phrase that she doesn't understand:

term of art
virtual warehousing of the young
concepts
precepts
index of my badness
hazing
predilection
paradigm
the Stoics

Artificially grouped together like this, they could be handed out to students as a vocab test. Over the course of the play's 90-odd minutes, they have a much subtler, cumulative effect on an audience, as Carol's shifting response to words whose meaning she cannot grasp becomes another symbol of the transfer of power.

Initially, she is able only to parrot the words as questions, but, partly with the help of her group, she acquires, step by step, the confidence to assert rather than apologise for her ignorance, and to challenge John's use of those words. The Carol of Act One would have followed John saying in Act Two that he is 'always looking for a *paradigm*' by saying 'Paradigm?'. Instead, we hear:

CAROL: I don't know what a paradigm is.
JOHN: It's a model.
CAROL: Then why can't you use that word? (p. 45)

She is, in effect, convicting John for inhibiting communication, by not suiting his language to his audience, and she goes on to nail him for a repeat offence in Act Three:

JOHN: And what would transpire.
CAROL: Transpire?
JOHN: Yes.
CAROL: 'Happen?'
JOHN: Yes.
CAROL: Then *say* it. For Christ's sake. (p. 66)

Once again, they are both right. John for wanting to use language as a precise instrument; Carol for complaining that he prevents her from understanding him by not making allowances for her comparatively poor grasp of language. As Michael Feingold wrote in his review of *Oleanna* in New York's *Village Voice*: 'If the student seems, at the start, hopelessly dense, it's clear soon enough that the teacher's choppy elliptical discourse, full of dubious concepts taken for granted, is one reason for her inability to grasp the material.'

There is occasionally a deliberate inconsistency in Carol's linguistic transformation. It will strike some in the audience as odd, to say the least, that the inarticulate young woman of Act One, is suddenly able to reproach John for remarks that 'countenance continuation of that method of thought'. *Financial Times* critic Malcolm Rutherford put it well: 'Carol picks up the language first used by the professor, though without the understanding' – and one of the most telling couplets in the play comes when John has noticed the change in her language:

JOHN: Can't you tell me in your own words?
CAROL: Those are my own words. (*Pause*) (p. 49)

The pause leaves her response hanging in the air: confident or defensive? It is very tempting to infer, as John does, that Carol is merely parroting the arguments and terminology that she has heard at group meetings (this was certainly Lia Williams's interpretation of Carol's transformation; see p. 1).

At times, Carol's linguistic education through the course of the play calls to mind Shakespeare's *The Tempest*, in which the island savage, Caliban, has been ensnared by Prospero. His master teaches him English, but he remains a slave, so what use is language to him?

> CALIBAN [*to Prospero*]: You taught me these words and my
> profit on't is that I know how to curse. (I, ii, l. 363)

Carol may have adopted John's over-elaborate vocabulary, but by the end of the play the only 'profit' it has brought her is violent assault and the illusion of liberation.

JOHN: *Get the fuck out of my office*

In several of Mamet's other plays, notably *American Buffalo* and *Sexual Perversity in Chicago*, expletives are part of the characters' standard vocabulary, with 'fuck' used so liberally that for the characters and audience the word has stock, rather than shock value. It may offend, but this is simply how these people talk.

In *Oleanna*, however, with so much of John's dialogue coated in a veneer of academic civility, the use of 'foul language' would be wholly inappropriate. That it intrudes on only three occasions gives each one great dramatic value.

The first, in Act One, has John describing himself as 'a fuck-up' during his speech about his educational inadequacies as a boy and he probably says it to ingratiate himself with Carol, adopting the sort of colloquialism that students might use among themselves.

At the end of Act Three, however, Mamet has this highly educated man resort to 'offensive' language as the prelude and accompaniment to physical violence. He tells Carol to 'Get the fuck out of my office' (p. 75) after she's asked for the removal of his book from the university syllabus and then, after knocking her to the floor: 'I wouldn't touch you with a ten-foot pole. You little *cunt* . . .' (p. 79).

That 'cunt' is the signal for him to lower the chair that he was about to bring down on Carol, suggesting that he may be as shocked at the word as at the violence. This articulate man has been reduced to using a word that retains a far greater potential to offend than 'fuck'. Audiences who recall the male protagonists within Mamet's work may associate the word with a misogynist like Bernard Litko in *Sexual Perversity in Chicago*, dismissing a woman who's rejected his advances as follows:

> BERNARD: I don't have better ways to spend my off hours than to listen to some nowhere cunt try out cute bits on me? I mean why don't you just clean up your fucking act, Missy. (*Mamet Plays: 1*, p. 59)

Or perhaps the eponymous hero of *Edmond*, who calls the woman with whom he's tried and failed to strike up a conversation on a subway platform 'You *cunt*', just a few minutes before he murders a waitress, Glenna. John's descent into violence is linguistic as well as physical.

CAROL: *Don't call your wife 'baby'*
There is a shocking irony in the fact that the word that triggers the climactic violence – 'baby' – is the simplest of the many terms that Carol has questioned or challenged earlier in the play. Her objection to the word is consistent with her earlier defence of the female member of the tenure committee whom John carelessly brands as one of the 'Good Men and True', or the fellow students whom he addresses as 'dear'. To her, and to some in the audience, 'baby' is another example of a powerful man using a term demeaning to women. To John, it is a term of endearment reserved for the woman he loves and it appears that he has been pushed over the boundary separating him from violent action because Carol has crossed another boundary: the one separating his professional life from his personal life.

So much of their conversation has been devoted to discussing the use of language in an institutional context, a miniature society governed, as Carol is always so keen to point out, by rules, and in which every member has the right not to be demeaned or patronised by another's language or actions. When he attacks Carol, the trigger word suggests that John is at least in part defending his right to use whatever language he chooses in the domestic sphere.

Carol

Oleanna's three-part structure corresponds to the transformation in Carol: from the passive, insecure figure of Act One, to the defiant accuser of Act Two and the assured and manipulative prosecutor of Act Three. If Mamet is to make these changes convincing, then he and the actress playing Carol must use Act One to establish how high the stakes are for her as a student in pursuit of a definite goal, and how deeply her faith in the university system runs. The depth of that faith must provide the dramatic justification for the extremity of her reaction when threatened.

In Act One, Carol is overwhelmed by a belief in her own ignorance and her inability to do the right thing, and Mamet establishes these twin pillars of her character in the first few moments after John's opening phone call. In her very first line ('What is a "term of art"?') we see her depending on John to explain the meaning of words, as she will do time and again (see p. xl), and her instinctive reaction is to assume that she's to blame for the situation.

CAROL: Did ... did I ... Did I say something wr ... (p. 3)

Her self-esteem is so low that in the opening exchanges her most 'assertive' line is to tell John that he does not have to apologise for appearing distracted.

In his portrayal of Carol's educational insecurity, Mamet taps into a universal experience that should resonate with every member of the audience wherever the play is staged – the uncomfortable, even frightening childhood memory of our own incomprehension in the classroom, regardless of age or subject, and our empathy (or contempt?) for the members of our class who struggled to grasp something that came to us more easily.

We all recall how isolated and vulnerable this made us or our classmates feel. In particular there's nothing more humiliating than having your words read back at you, as John does in quoting from Carol's paper, and this particular moment helped Lia Williams to tap into Carol's state of mind during Oleanna rehearsals: 'I drew a lot of Carol either from observing other children being annihilated or from my own memories of a maths teacher I had who was a complete bastard and who used to humiliate me by writing my incorrect answers up on the board. Or he'd tear up the work that I'd spent three hours sobbing over the night before because I couldn't do it. So for me Carol was completely three-dimensional and utterly recognisable, not extraordinary or strange or evil.'

Carol's sense of her own stupidity is matched by her absolute faith in the omniscience of her teachers, and of John in particular, established instantly when she insists that he could never forget the meaning of a word; she's the one who can't even grasp meanings, let alone have an opportunity to forget what she's learned.

Her third conviction is that there is a set pattern of behaviour for the diligent student:

> CAROL: I sit in class I . . . (*She holds up her notebook.*) I take notes . . .

And then:

> I'm doing what I'm told, I bought your book, I read your . . .

But she finds that following the rules is not enough to get by, and we reach the root of her problem:

> CAROL: *The language*, the 'things' that you say . . . (p. 6)

As she fights against John's constant interruptions, Mamet defines Carol initially through her intellectual and educational problems, then sketches in the social and economic factors that are such a potent influence on her expectations of the university system and on her subsequent behaviour:

> CAROL: I come from a different *social* . . . a different *economic* . . . (p. 8)

She is labouring under the additional weight of parental expectation of her success ('How can I go back and tell them the *grades* that I . . .') and we conclude that Carol is certainly not a product of private school (as John intends his son to be), and also, perhaps, that her parents did not go to university and have invested correspondingly great hopes in her.

At Carol's stage in life, our identities are to a large extent defined by our family backgrounds, and when John fails to acknowledge the importance of Carol's personal circumstances she asks 'Does that mean nothing?'. If John feels that where she comes from is of no significance, isn't he at least partially denying her an identity?

Though Mamet does not dwell for long on Carol's 'back story', the opening exchanges were of great use to Lia Williams: 'We discovered that she'd had a struggle and that she arrives into the university and into the play with an inferiority complex which I think was very real. The university environment was quite alien to her.'

Carol's inferiority complex – the weighty chip on her shoulder – will be echoed more forcefully in Act Two ('You've no idea what it cost me to come to this school') and in Act Three when she talks of the economic and sexual prejudices and humiliations that she overcame to gain a place at the university. And yet, gaining a place is not even half the battle; nor is her faith in higher education an end in itself. She must pass John's course in order 'to get on in the world'. We don't know if she has any idea yet of what she will do in the world, but it is essential to get through this stage, secure a place at graduate school and then the well-paid job that will lift her clear of her background for ever.

There is something obsessive about her pursuit of this goal ('I *have* to pass this course'); her pleading ('Teach me, teach me') is almost a litany. In the Royal Court production, Lia Williams used Carol's notebook as a combination of bible and rosary (whereas in Acts Two and Three Carol's notes become a weapon rather than a crutch) and her posture suggested that of a supplicant in search of absolution. The quasi-religious aspect of John's and Carol's relationship has begun to emerge even before he launches into the 'parable' of the airline pilot, or talks of belief in higher education as 'an article of faith'. And in Act Three Carol will attack him for assuming and abusing his God-like powers over his students.

For John to tell her in her hour of need 'It's just a course, it's just a book' and to offer to make her final grade an 'A' in defiance of the 'rules' is to deny Carol's faith in her present and her future; it is akin to the priest who tells a devout member of his congregation 'There is no God'.

Through Carol, Mamet shows that what defines you and roots you in a university environment are your grades. Ultimately, therefore, what Carol wants from the first meeting is to know about her grade. Working her way out of 'the need to fail' and reaching a genuine understanding of John's course can wait.

If we have begun to see Carol's and John's relationship as pupil/teacher and parishioner/priest, then Mamet also suggests a sexual connotation, through the ambiguity of key lines:

> CAROL: But then, what am I doing here . . . ? . . . when nobody wants me, and . . . (p. 14)

followed soon afterwards by 'Why would you want to be personal with me?' and 'Why would you like me?' Here is someone as unaccustomed to people saying they like her, on any level, as she is accustomed to feeling stupid.

The undercurrent of the exchange is ripe for sexual misinterpretation, with John saying 'Let's start over' as though they were lovers patching up a quarrel, and suggesting additional private meetings, and Carol herself using a phrase that a million girlfriends utter every week: 'I don't understand you' (as against her earlier variations on 'I don't understand your language').

Through all this, the actress must at least suggest that Carol is, in the shocking self-definition of Act Three, a 'frightened, repressed, confused, I don't know, abandoned young thing of some doubtful sexuality'.

The economy with which Mamet conveys Carol's vulnerability at all levels – intellectual, social and sexual – makes equally plausible John's terrible error in putting a comforting arm around her, and his multiple roles (teacher, father-figure, priest, lover?) explain why she is driven to confess that her failure in college has a moral and spiritual dimension:

> CAROL: I'm bad. (*Pause*) Oh, God. (p. 38)

It's a short step from here to 'Forgive me, father, for I have sinned.'

Like a Catholic in the confessional, or a lover in bed, she is

about to tell John a secret that no one else knows, which is
why the phone interruption – and John's decision to pick up
the phone – is such a crushing moment, compounded by the
revelation of the surprise party.

By now, we have formed a clear picture of what's missing in
Carol's life outside the lecture hall, so we can imagine her
baffled envy of John's life, in which there are people so proud
of you that they throw a surprise party. What she's thinking
about is going home to tell her parents that she's failed.
'They're proud of you' she tells him – and the unspoken second
half of the line is 'but no one is going to be proud of me'.

Act One ends, therefore, with John at his highest point and
Carol at her lowest. All the questions she brought to his office
are unanswered, and she's more confused than when she came
in.

By this point, Mamet has also established two other aspects
of Carol's make-up that have a major bearing on her behaviour
in Acts Two and Three. Firstly, that while she may think that
she's stupid and may not *understand* his language, she is a
grade A listener, able to throw John's words back at him either
from memory ('You said, 'What can that mean?' '), or from
the almost obsessively made notes. Her note-taking is both
entirely in character with her behaviour in Act One and serves
to establish the credibility of the notes that she has evidently
been taking throughout the semester ('The twelfth: "Have a
good day, dear." ' etc.).

If she has been keeping dated records of John's remarks in
class then she may have been planning to make a complaint
against him for some time. This in turn could indicate that she
comes to his office to set him up and that her vulnerability in
the opening scene might be at least partly an act, designed to
provoke John into behaviour that will justify a more serious
complaint. However the film version of *Oleanna* (see p. lxix)
shows Carol going to see John on impulse, whatever the
intention behind her prior note-taking may be.

Despite being so bound up in her own individual concerns,
she has a sense of her position as part of a wider community:

CAROL: There are *people* out there. People who came *here*. To
know something they didn't *know*. Who *came* here. To be

helped. To be *helped*. So someone would *help* them. (p. 12)

And, later, when she challenges John for his dismissal of higher education: 'But how do they feel? Being told they're wasting their time?' (p. 35). These are important pointers towards her shift from passive, struggling member of that community to active defender of its rights in Acts Two and Three (see also p. xxxv):

> CAROL: Whatever you've done to me – to the extent that you've done it to *me*, do you know, rather than to me as a *student*, and, so, to the student body, is contained in my report. To the tenure committee. (p. 47)

Then: '. . . you hold our confusion as a *joke*, and our hopes and efforts with it.'

In Acts Two and Three she appears to have a more secure sense of her identity as part of the community and, more particularly, her group, than as an individual, so much so that she will eventually ask John to accept that 'What I feel is irrelevant'; she partially denies her individuality as John did in Act One.

We cannot help questioning whether we are seeing the 'real' Carol in Acts Two and Three, or someone who has merely exchanged one false god (John) for another (her group), replacing the doctrine of absolute belief in higher education with a zealous condemnation of that same system. She may believe what she says when she tells John: 'I don't think that I need your help. I don't think that I need anything that you have' but if so, it's only because she now needs the group's help instead. Was the report as much her own work as the essay that John tears apart in Act One, or was it embellished by the group, based on her oral testimony?

The change is so pronounced that several British theatre critics singled out Carol's transformation as the least convincing aspect of *Oleanna*'s London production. Paul Taylor in the *Independent* questioned the plausibility of her 'hefty personality rethink'; Jane Edwardes in *Time Out* felt that the newly confident Carol was 'too different for credibility' and John Gross in the *Sunday Telegraph* said 'the transformation of Carol from mumbling lost soul to fluent ideologue is too rapid and extreme'.

The change may seem more credible if you believe that Carol begins Act One intent on making a complaint about John. If her vulnerability in the first meeting is partly an act then perhaps the 'real' Carol comes through in the second and third meetings. Maybe we never see the 'real' Carol at all. The 'if's, 'but's and 'maybe's prompted by her behaviour go some way to explaining why *Oleanna* is so provocative and divisive a play, painted in umpteen shades of grey, where a lesser dramatist would provide us with comforting black and white, villain and victim.

Lia Williams believed that the change in Carol could be explained as follows: 'Through the play she begins to understand a great deal of herself and she has great tenacity and if she believes in a thing, whether it's right or wrong, she hangs on to it like a mutt hanging on to a pair of trousers. She will not be shaken off, she discovers that about herself during One, goes away, discovers it some more, is fed by her group, then comes back and hangs on even harder in Two. And the same happens between Two and Three.

'I think she recognised that she was getting a bit of attention, probably repeated to the group something that John had said to her in One, which probably silenced them all a bit. Once that happened they riled her and nudged her forward, not necessarily for her own well-being. She saw a chance to be part of something; to be recognised and for somebody to listen to her made her feel good. To be part of a group is probably a new experience for her and one she won't let go of. So I'd imagine that fed itself. They fed her. That spurred her to go back in there. She had a temporary popularity which she'd never experienced before and rather liked it. Maybe she didn't think beyond that.'

Having built up this impression of her dependence on the group, Mamet also invites us to question whether Carol believes, deep down, that she has been the victim of attempted rape and whether she would be pursuing the case against John so vigorously without the group's support:

> CAROL: My Group has told your lawyer that we may pursue criminal charges . . .

JOHN: . . . no . . .

CAROL: . . . under the statute, I am told it was battery.

JOHN: . . . no . . .

CAROL: Yes. And attempted rape. That's right. (p. 78)

Is she doing what she's been told, not what she feels is right?

Williams says that she 'always struggled with the rape issue. I remember looking at the climax of Two and asking Harold Pinter [director] "What is this?" He'd very clearly say "It's an invasion of your space, your territory, therefore it's rape." But I always felt that it was Mamet pushing me a little too far in terms of setting this girl up for a fall. But I'd also get letters from women and have conversations with women who would say to me "It wasn't invited or asked for. Absolutely it's rape." '

The terrible irony of *Oleanna*'s climax is that the possibly over-inflated allegation of attempted rape and battery, and the new-found confidence that charge gives Carol, ultimately provoke the genuine physical assault that ensures neither party emerges victorious.

Williams's experience of the part confirms the sense in which Carol becomes as much a victim of her new-found power as she was a victim of her powerlessness in Act One. 'You give somebody like that power and they don't know what to do with it – she's never had those feelings before. The power that she exerts on John is only what she's observed him doing to her. She becomes what people have influenced her to become. I have immense sympathy for her, because she becomes monstrous, but she's still completely human.'

John

I wanted to show a man who was arrogant, pompous, self-obsessed, in love with the sound of his own voice, always coming back to himself when discussing someone else's problems and never listening. But, at the same time, he is totally unaware of all these facts, and genuinely believes he is acting for the best. (David Suchet on playing John, interviewed in the *Daily Telegraph*, September 1993)

Why doesn't John leave the office after the opening phone call with Grace? This is the most pressing of the many questions prompted by his behaviour, and relates to his first and greatest mistake (without which, of course, we do not have a play).

'His wife wants him home, so why doesn't he go? That in itself is slightly suspect,' suggests Suchet. 'On one level, he stays because he doesn't want anybody, including Carol, to talk badly about him. He's a basically weak man who is hoist by his own petard, by trying so hard to be nice.' He appears to care less about the house purchase than about Carol and how he might help her – but everything that we see him say and do in Act One indicates that the leading motive for staying may be that the meeting provides an irresistible opportunity to exercise power over a student.

The next question is why, having made the decision to stay, doesn't John listen more attentively and do more to help Carol? Because, on all the available evidence, he's a terrible teacher – a flaw that Mamet identifies in the opening exchanges as economically as he establishes Carol's insecurity. Rather than asking her what she wants to talk about he asks the obviously ridiculous question of whether she wants the definition of 'a term of art' to be the topic of the meeting. There's no attempt to put her at her ease, and the tone of Act One has been set.

Suchet saw John's 'failure to listen' as perhaps the greatest single flaw in his make-up, and much of *Oleanna*'s uneasy comedy stems from John's emphasis on the importance of Carol using her own words instead of her notes, while never letting her say what she wants to. One of the most uncomfortably amusing examples is on p. 30, when his encouraging 'That's right! Speak up!' is itself one of his umpteen interruptions. After what we observe in Act One, his plaintive 'If you would hear me out', in Act Three, could hardly be more ironic.

Rather than seek the cause of Carol's problems or accept that his complex treatment of the concepts and precepts may have helped to cause her confusion, he chooses, in characteristically solipsistic and self-contradictory fashion, to play the empathy card. He wants to be looked up to as an authority figure but also wants her to believe that he has suffered as she suffers.

John is like the man on a blind date who talks about himself for an hour and then apologises: 'That's enough about me. What do you think of me?' His arrogance and love of the sound of his own voice render him as incapable of a balanced two-way conversation as the tongue-tied Carol. All too often, John sounds as though he is on the podium of a lecture hall, as when Carol quotes 'virtual warehousing of the young' from his book and he slips effortlessly into the kind of definition that would be better suited to some earnest TV discussion programme than a one-on-one tutorial with an anxious, vulnerable student. He appears to have no notion of the pastoral care that a good college professor knows should accompany intellectual rigour if students are to realise their potential.

Mamet brilliantly distils both John's professional vanity and his utter disregard for Carol into the following exchange on p. 33:

> JOHN: What might be some reasons for pursuit of higher education?
> *One:* A love of learning.
> *Two:* The wish for mastery of a skill.
> *Three:* For economic betterment.
> (*Stops. Makes a note.*)
> CAROL: I'm keeping you.
> JOHN: One moment. I have to make a note . . .
> CAROL: It's something that I said?
> JOHN: No, we're buying a house.

He interrupts the lecture, but, naturally, the break is not prompted by something she has said, he's thinking 'Aha, this is good stuff – I can use this in a lecture or a journal article.' Carol might as well not be there, and there's something painfully redundant in his asking 'does this interest you?'. As if he cares.

Even under threat, John is never happier than when he is the subject of the lecture, notably in the childhood and teenage reminiscences of Act One, or the long speech at the start of Act Two. His love for 'the aspect of performance' in academic life contributes to his downfall because he views his job as a one-man show; we perceive that it's a self-indulgent performance from which his audience/students have little to gain and to which they contribute even less.

The tactics of Carol's counter-attack are of course dubious in the extreme, but when she rebukes John for dismissing higher education as 'hazing' while exploiting the system for his own gain, his guilt is beyond question. Mamet equips him with what *Sunday Times* critic John Peter succinctly identified as 'the ghastly egomaniacal sincerity of the teacher who does not really believe in teaching but relishes the opportunity to lay down the law'.

By the end of Act One we are also bound to ask ourselves, 'Does John want to have sex with Carol?' However violent his ultimate denial of any sexual interest in her ('I wouldn't touch you with a ten-foot pole'), we cannot help believing that part of him likes the idea of being, in the committee's damning phrase, 'closeted with a student' after hours. There is sufficient ambiguity in his rejection of teacher-student 'strictures' for us to feel that the idea of Carol having a crush on him and of a secret 'sex for an A-grade' arrangement holds a certain appeal, though probably more to his vanity than his libido. 'I think that he might have been capable of an affair with a student,' suggests David Suchet, 'but I don't know that he'd have gone the whole way because I don't know that he could have handled the consequences.'

Mamet has John commit a sequence of mistakes. Each error compounds the previous one, and each is prompted more by John's character flaws than by Carol's actions. Several arise from his tendency to speak before he thinks, firstly when he tells Carol: 'You're an incredibly bright girl' only a few moments before he reads back an essay that he clearly believes to have been written by an idiot. When Carol says 'I'm stupid' he should, at least for consistency's sake, remind her that she's 'incredibly bright', but all he can manage is 'No one thinks you're stupid'.

When he tells her 'Look. Look. I'm not your *father*', we, like Carol, are jolted by the crassness of the remark; and later in the scene he will manage to contradict himself while still patronising her – 'I'm talking to you as I'd talk to my son' – even though his son ('the yard for the boy') is evidently much younger than Carol. That one sentence is ripe with self-contradiction, affected intimacy *and* condescension – three of John's worst traits, all attacked and exploited by Carol in Acts Two and Three. 'He sounds patronising to Carol and to the audience, but not to himself,' Suchet believes. 'He thinks he's doing the right thing, by saying he's on her level, even though he's clearly not.'

The man who in Act Two will talk of 'my unflinching concern for my students' dignity' is the same man whom we've seen humiliating Carol by reading out her essay in Act One (in a stunning piece of improvisation for the Royal Court production, Suchet had John accentuate Carol's humiliation by tearing the essay in half when John says 'Forget about the paper'). He professes to like her but still abandons her at her lowest ebb in Act One, without apology, to head off to his surprise party. He wants to convince her that there are '*norms*' of behaviour, but advocates breaking college rules.

In the midst of so much self-contradiction, John's only consistent trait is his denial of responsibility, no matter what specific charge Carol makes. He did not call her stupid; the language of his books and lectures is not too complicated; the hand on her shoulder did not carry sexual content; he did not intend to demean the female member of the tenure committee and so on. That's why the exchange on p. 68 is so quietly shocking:

> CAROL: You think I am a frightened, repressed, confused, I don't know, abandoned young thing of some doubtful sexuality, who wants, power and revenge. (*Pause*) *Don't* you? (*Pause*)
> JOHN: Yes. I do. (*Pause*)
> CAROL: Isn't that better? And I feel that that is the first moment which you've treated me with respect. For you told me the truth.

When she goes on to ask if he hates her and he again says yes, those two affirmatives, after so many vehement denials, bring tremendous relief to him, to Carol and also to the audience. Here at last, we think, is direct and successful communication, both parties saying what they really mean; at least they can agree that John hates her.

The admission of hatred is a significant step on the journey to John's self-knowledge as tragic hero (touched on on pp. xxviii–xxxi). The John of Acts One and Two has been incapable of accepting that 'there is much good' in what Carol has been talking about, as he now can, however grudgingly, or of accepting that he is in any way 'deficient'.

But self-knowledge for the hero means an acceptance of responsibility and of his flaws, not a complete denial of the identity and roles in which he has hitherto believed so absolutely. For John to read the group's demands is one thing, but to endorse their censorship of the reading list and sign their statement would mean accepting that there is good in *everything* that Carol says; that nothing he has done as a teacher has had value; that freedom of thought and speech are not worth defending.

When he says 'I don't know what I was thinking of' (p. 76) he is apologising to himself for contemplating surrender. He owes Carol a debt because she's made him see how his behaviour has contributed to the situation, however inadvertently. His role now is to accept his destruction in order to be true to himself – flaws and all.

It is here that John most resembles John Proctor, the hero of Arthur Miller's tragedy, *The Crucible* (1953), in more than just name. Miller's play, set during the witch trials in Salem, Massachusetts, in 1692, is an allegorical response to the 1950s anti-communist witch-hunt led in America by Senator Joe McCarthy (commonly referred to as McCarthyism), just as *Oleanna* is Mamet's response to the McCarthyite tendencies of political correctness in the 1990s.

Proctor is a devoted husband and father who has committed adultery with his housemaid, Abigail (a vulnerable, vengeful young woman not unlike Carol), and it is her fury at being rejected by him that sets off the witch-hunt that will destroy him. At the play's climax, Proctor perjures himself to save his life, by pretending that he has seen the Devil (this was Miller's metaphor for membership of the Communist party, the un-American activity for which McCarthy persecuted thousands). Proctor is then ordered to sign a written confession and does so, but he refuses to hand it over to the judge to be displayed before the whole town. Why?

> PROCTOR (*with a cry of his soul*): Because it is my name! Because I cannot have another in my life! Because I lie and sign myself to lies! ... How may I live without my name? (Penguin Modern Classics, pp. 124-5)

He then tears up the confession, knowing that he will hang, and the realisation that, despite his mistakes and compromises he has remained true to himself enables him to say: 'Now I do see some shred of goodness in John Proctor.'

Mamet's John refuses to save himself by signing the statement prepared by Carol's group because he, too, cannot bear the idea of others seeing his name attached to a lie, and he echoes Proctor:

> JOHN: It's my *name* on the door, and *I* teach the class, and that's what I do. I've got a book with my name on it. And my son will *see* that *book* someday [. . .] And I have a *responsibility* . . . to *myself*, to my *son*, to my *profession* . . . (p. 76)

He can face his fate with head held high, as Proctor faces his, and it's possible to imagine 'Go to *hell*, and they can do whatever they want to me' as the curtain line of a play that would give John a victory of sorts.

Yet Mamet pushes both characters even further. Carol extends her PC doctrine into John's personal life, with the provocative 'Don't call your wife "baby"', and John responds with impulsive violence – this time acting without thought after so many thoughtless remarks.

Part of John's tragedy is that he is driven to a point where, in resorting to violence, he temporarily forgets the responsibilities and values that define him.

Other characters

Imagine an alternative stage version of *Oleanna*, opened out
from the two-hander format to include scenes that must or
might have taken place before Act One, between Two and
Three and after Three. The majority of the off-stage characters
referred to by Carol and John have the potential to play crucial
supporting roles in this expanded drama, because they all exert
a powerful influence on John and Carol and on our
understanding of their behaviour.

With great economy, Mamet supplies just enough clues from
which each audience member can form a mental picture of
these people. Grace and Carol's group, in particular, are sure to
have featured in the furious post-performance arguments that
raged during the original American and British runs of *Oleanna*
(see p. lxv).

John's wife and son
Audience views of John will be shaped in part by how they
picture his family and his relationships with them.

Do we conclude, for instance, that Grace is a fellow
academic or a high-flyer in another profession? Is she 'merely' a
housewife and mother? Do we agree with Carol, for whom
Grace is just another symbol of John's ill-gotten status:

> CAROL: You worked twenty years for the right to *insult* me.
> And you feel entitled to be *paid* for it. Your Home. Your
> Wife . . . Your sweet 'deposit' on your house . . . (p. 65)

As always in *Oleanna*, Mamet does not allow us the comfort
of a clear-cut answer to these questions, but he does enable us
to appreciate how Grace is caught in the crossfire of the battle
between her husband and his student.

Grace's unheard voice at the end of the telephone and her
impatient presence hover throughout Act One. She twice
declares her love for John in the opening phone call and insists
that he say the same to her. She is evidently so proud of his
promotion – and, by extension, so happy at the imminent new
stage in their shared life – that she has gone to the trouble of
organising the surprise party, so we may well carry into the

interval between Acts One and Two an image of Grace as the delighted party hostess, as secure of her place in the world as John is of his.

Contrast this rose-tinted opening with the image of her at home that we take from the couple's final phone conversation (the briefest they have): desperate for John's return after he has been away from home for two days and stunned by the news that he may be guilty of attempted rape.

Despite her passive role in the drama, she inadvertently becomes the catalyst for John's violence, when Carol chastises him for calling his wife 'baby'. Would Grace herself see this, as Carol does, as a demeaning epithet, or as a term of endearment between loving equals? Though we never even hear her voice, Grace provides a counterpoint to Carol in our judgment of John's treatment of women.

As for John's son, Mamet does not even reveal his age or name, but in just one, immensely evocative phrase in the opening phone conversation – John's 'the yard for the boy' – he conjures up in our minds an image of what we think John and his family are about to gain, and therefore what he stands to lose: a domestic Oleanna.

We may see the boy as blessed with a father who wants only the best for him, sending him to private school in the hope of providing him with teachers more considerate than his own. We may condemn John for using his son to perpetuate an educational élite, but we should leave the theatre viewing the boy as a victim. After John has been dismissed and disgraced there will surely be neither private school nor yard for the boy. The destruction of John's career may also destroy an apparently happy and loving family.

Jerry

John's relationship with his lawyer does not extend much beyond the exchange of information and instructions, yet their familiarity adds another layer to Carol's and our view of John's comfortable upper-middle-class existence: on first-name terms with another professional, on whom he thinks he can depend to resolve any problem.

The tenure committee

The committee occupy a unique position within the world of *Oleanna*, as the only people to have power over John and Carol. The committee are both judge and jury. If they were to dismiss Carol's complaints, her reputation within the university would be tainted; by upholding them they destroy John's career.

We may form an opinion of the committee based on John's arrogance towards them ('The Bad Tenure Committee' and 'the Great Tenure Committee'; 'The Tenure Committee, Good Men and True . . .'), or we may share Carol's faith in their absolute authority and impartiality. Many will undoubtedly want to ask: 'Why do they believe her version of events?'

Carol's parents

As with John's son, the economy of Mamet's writing is such that one line:

> CAROL: How can I go back and tell them the *grades* that I . . .

is sufficient to conjure up a vivid domestic scene: a daughter from a lowly socio-economic background returns home from college to disappoint her expectant parents. By the end of the play, the seed planted by that one line and the tense little exchange when John tells Carol 'I'm not your father' should also make us consider how her parents might react to Carol's notoriety within and beyond the university after she has made the rape claim.

Carol's group

Mamet might have given Carol's group a label – 'The Students Coalition', perhaps – but their politically correct agenda and the almost cult-like influence they exert over Carol appear all the more dangerous because they remain nameless and nebulous. John has Grace and Jerry; Carol has only 'the people I've been talking to'. Is it a mixed group, or all-female? Might it include some of John's teaching colleagues?

Mamet invites the audience to project on to the group their

own prejudices about what such collectives are like and Lia
Williams remembers how *Oleanna*'s London audiences would
'instantly pass judgment' on the group as soon as Carol
mentioned them: 'You could feel people nodding to themselves
as if to say "A group like that must be a nightmare so we
must judge Carol accordingly". Whereas John could talk about
the tenure committee and the audience wouldn't judge him.'

Oleanna in performance

Every theatre script becomes a different entity when it is
performed rather than read, but I know of few cases where
that differential is as pronounced as with *Oleanna*. If you read
it without having seen it in a packed theatre it is impossible
fully to appreciate its power to grip and provoke an audience,
the cumulative effect of John's and Carol's failure to
communicate, the tension that builds in the awkward silences,
the breathtaking shock of the final assault.

The Royal Court production
Mamet had directed the American production himself but in
London that job went to the playwright Harold Pinter, to
whom Mamet had dedicated the published script of *Glengarry
Glen Ross* (Pinter was instrumental in arranging that play's
première at the National Theatre in September 1983) and of
whom Mamet has said: 'He was always a hero of mine and
really was responsible to a large extent for me starting to
write.'

As John, Pinter cast David Suchet, a vastly experienced actor
who had played roles as diverse as Iago and Timon of Athens
for the Royal Shakespeare Company, as well as Hercule Poirot
on television. Carol was played by Lia Williams, a slightly
built, fair-haired actress for whom this was a breakthrough
stage role. Physically and vocally they were well-matched:
Suchet a robust, comfortably-built figure with well-groomed
hair, old enough to be Williams's father but not too old for us
to imagine him as lover to this apparently frail, cowed young
woman. Suchet adopted the smooth New England accent and

rhetorical assurance of the professional speaker; Williams used an accent that suggested a run-down Bronx apartment block.

The contrast was enhanced by their costumes. In Act One, Carol wore jeans, white blouse and trainers and a sweater – a figure-hiding, almost asexual combination. But in Act Three, the long blonde hair that had hung down on both sides of her head was now brushed back to one side and she wore a soft, printed skirt and a black T-shirt, creating a discreetly but unmistakably sexy impression. 'Harold and I instinctively felt that Carol would now be feminine and soft,' recalls Williams, 'but we didn't want her to look like a siren.'

John starts off casually dressed in beige slacks and polo shirt, no tie, his sports jacket hung over the back of his chair – the classic 'uniform' of the preppy American college professor. Says Suchet: 'It helped to show that he was at ease, that the office was his place.' But for Acts Two and Three he changed into a grey, three-piece check suit that would not have looked out of place on a Wall Street banker or lawyer. 'Wearing the suit was John's way of protecting himself,' says Suchet, 'creating a barrier against Carol that wasn't there when he was dressed down in One.'

The set designer, Eileen Diss, furnished John with a spacious office that filled the Royal Court stage. His large desk (with neatly arranged piles of correspondence and documents on it, but no computer) was upstage right, with a heavy, wooden swivel chair behind it. There was one plain, straight-backed chair in front of the desk, centre stage, and another downstage right, with a pair of two-seater benches, one upstage left, the other downstage left.

The characters' movements within the office were meticulously choreographed so that the stage picture always reflected the shifting dynamics in their relationship. For example, in Act One, John and Carol were often very close together, mostly seated across the desk from each other, or on the downstage left bench (to which Suchet led Williams when John consoles Carol towards the end of the act). At the start of Act Two, however, the teacher-pupil rift that has opened between the two meetings was instantly emphasised by having the greatest possible distance between the actors: Williams was on the downstage left bench, Suchet stood upstage right.

The movements that evolved in rehearsal illustrate why Mamet believes that detailed, scripted stage directions are often redundant. 'When you write stage directions,' he told John Lahr, 'unless they're absolutely essential for the understanding of the action of the play ("He leaves"; "She shoots him") something else is going to happen when the actors and directors get them on the stage' (*Paris Review* 39, no. 142, Spring 1997). For example, in Act One, Williams twice stood up and made as if to leave the room (first after referring to her socio-economic background, then when John takes his first phone call from Jerry), adding to our sense of her unease and the feeling that the meeting could end at any moment.

'The body language and positioning speak so strongly to an audience, especially if there are only two people on stage,' says Suchet. Williams remembers: 'We spent a lot of time in rehearsal actually shedding movement, rather than adding it, so that when we did move it was crucially important to the text and what we were trying to say at that moment in time.'

Perhaps the most effective unscripted idea was the erection of an invisible barrier between John and Carol, along the line of John's desk. In Act One, the area behind this line was exclusively John's territory, allowing Suchet complete freedom of movement, while Williams was confined to the area to the left of the desk and for most of the scene to the chair in front of it. Control of the stage/office reflected control of the meeting.

The desk became the central symbol of John's power, never more so than at the moment in Act One when John pleads with Carol to sit down, switches to his most ingratiating mode and says 'I'll tell you a story about myself'. Suchet stood looming over Williams, hands in pockets, his crotch close to her eyeline – the picture of confident supremacy, intellectual and sexual.

For Suchet 'that dividing line of the desk was the most important thing' in mapping the characters' movements. Only in Acts Two and Three did Williams come around to John's side of the room. To see her standing, in Act Two, as she criticised John for 'demeaning' the woman on the tenure committee, while he sat at his desk, was a clear physical signal that they were now approaching equal status.

Then, in Act Three, when Carol tells him that 'YOUR OWN ACTIONS' are to blame for his predicament it was John's turn to sit meekly (in the downstage right chair), his tentative posture, hands on knees, exactly like Carol's in Act One, while she sat nonchalantly on the edge of his desk. 'Her sitting on the desk – claiming it – was one of the most powerful moments in the play,' says Williams. The final visual reversal came in Carol's speech beginning 'Why do you hate me?' Williams bore down on Suchet and he raised his hands to halt her; a mirror image of John's approach towards Carol at the end of Act One.

The actors' interpretation of Mamet's stage direction – 'He goes over to her and puts his arm around her shoulder' – was also vital in determining audience responses to the question of whether the physical contact was 'devoid of sexual content'. Suchet gently tapped Williams's left shoulder with his left hand, three sets of three taps, then used his left palm to usher her towards the downstage left bench – to my eyes like a doctor leading a patient, utterly devoid of sexual intent. But as they sat side by side he had both of his hands on her left hand, which was resting on her left knee – a more ambiguous pose, possibly paternal, but also like that of a tentative couple in the early stages of courtship.

Suchet says that he could only play this as 'an innocent arm around the shoulder, to comfort someone who was crying', not as a sexual advance, even of the most surreptitious kind. Williams tried to play the moment as neutrally as possible. 'I certainly never wanted it to look like she was deliberately setting him up and inviting the physical comfort as something which she could then use against him.

'It was certainly never a conscious decision on our part to play the sexual tension between them, but it's there in the text – something coming from her as much as from him. I don't know whether that was about power or John as a father-figure, but there was a tension that grew within the scene and wrapped itself around these two people. I'm not sure that they could escape it, or wanted to escape – although if John and

Carol were here now they'd fiercely deny that.'

At every stage, Williams adds, they took great pains 'to create a balanced argument, an equal battle'. But as soon as the play was presented to an audience, cast and director were 'absolutely staggered by the fantastically violent reaction towards Carol' – something that had already happened in America.

Audience reactions

During the initial run of *Oleanna* in Cambridge, Massachusetts, a row filled with Harvard professors stood up at the end of one performance and booed. In New York, after a performance at which several people applauded John's assault on Carol, a woman stood up as the house lights came up and said, 'Let's find those guys who clapped.'

Mamet himself was shocked. 'I had never seen reactions like that in a theatre before,' he told American television interviewer Charlie Rose. 'Night after night and couple by couple, the people would split down the middle and it wouldn't always be by sex, and it wouldn't always be by age. But one or the other would say "I think he's right", "I think she's right".

'People suspend their disbelief for a second, they say "Okay, I'm going to watch a funny little story, and everything will be under my control". And then, because of the structure of the piece, because it moved so fast and it's so clear what each one wants next, and you get two-thirds of the way through the play, and you think you know what's going on. And all of a sudden it takes a turn that you don't want, and you find you've identified with one of the two ... and you start feeling like, "Wait, wait a second". It gets under people's skins not because of the issues, I think, but because of the drama involved in the two protagonists.'

The almost hysterical aggression shown towards his wife, Rebecca Pidgeon, as Carol, also shocked him (John was played by William H. Macy, one of Mamet's former students and a regular actor in his plays and films). 'I was always frightened that someone was going to attack her, come over the footlights and attack her,' he told John Lahr (*Paris Review*). The actress

Mary McCann, who succeeded Pidgeon as Carol, said that people in the audience 'look at me like an axe murderer'.

Audiences in Britain were no less vociferous. Suchet recalls a matinée at the Theatre Royal, Bath, during the production's pre-London tour, after which there was a question-and-answer session with the cast. A well-dressed elderly woman stood up and said: 'I'm a very mild woman, Mr Suchet, and I don't know what it was but, when you started to hit her, I nearly stood up and shouted "Kill the bitch!" and I find myself appalled by what I nearly did.'

Williams says that, once she'd overcome the initial shock, she realised 'what genius it takes to write a play that makes an audience think "Oh my God, I've just cheered a man's violence towards a woman". It's fantastic manipulation of an audience on Mamet's part.'

She was taken aback at how attentive audiences were, and how the tiniest detail could evoke a disproportionately large response. 'It was as if our sensibilities were heightened as actors and the audience's were, too. If I heard somebody sigh with exasperation at something that Carol said, or move to the edge of their seat with anticipation, it would affect my performance and it worked the other way around, with my gestures. In one preview, I was talking to John and I just gently moved a lick of hair back behind my ear, which I hadn't done in rehearsal. Harold saw this and said, "Don't move, because every move will be interpreted." I realised that everyday movements that one makes in real life without thinking just weren't acceptable in *Oleanna*. So I had to teach myself an extraordinary stillness. I had never known until *Oleanna* what it felt like to be so still on stage and how powerful that could be.

'An extraordinary thing happened one matinée. In Act Three, when Carol was standing over him and in the middle of her diatribe against him, my eye caught this woman, sitting near the front of the stalls, and she was breastfeeding her baby. I was so staggered by what I'd seen that it made me smile, just for a moment, which I never did in other performances. When it came to the fight I was annihilated by the audience, it got one of the biggest cheers of the run. Because of my inadvertent smile, the audience thought I had been laughing at the man I was destroying. It was such a tiny moment and it got this incredible reaction.'

What the critics said
A selection from British reviews of the Royal Court production:

'Mamet's new play heaves and edges towards its climax like a prolonged underground explosion . . . This is a play about power . . . a confrontation both between people and between values, brilliantly constructed and savagely even-handed.' (John Peter, *Sunday Times*)

'It is a powerful disturbing evening and will divide husband from wife, lover from lover, friend from friend wherever it is discussed.' (Jack Tinker, *Daily Mail*)

'*Oleanna* is a deeply uncomfortable drama. It demonstrates the pernicious workings of political correctness with almost clinical precision while showing how an apparently reasonable man can indeed become the violent monster of feminist demonology. The play will trouble the memory of all who see it like an itching, aching scab.' (Charles Spencer, *Daily Telegraph*)

'Rarely can there have been such a manipulative clarion call to men's baser instincts. It's a very uncomfortable equation between the rise of feminism and a decline in freedom of thought . . . I enjoyed the drama but I can't say that I feel there is much substance to Mamet's fears. Real men will love it.' (Jane Edwardes, *Time Out*)

'Mamet is not simply writing about the excesses of political correctness. He is not even purely concerned with a transference of power in American life, from the teacher to the pupil. What he has created is a superb mythic drama about the breaking of the social contract that makes all education possible . . . Mamet's point is that once people resort to ideological jargon or legalistic devices, then the whole idea of intellectual freedom breaks down.' (Michael Billington, *Guardian*)

Other newspaper coverage

Such was the controversy stirred up by *Oleanna* that newspaper coverage extended from the arts pages into the features sections. On 7 July 1993, a few days after the London production opened, the *Guardian* ran a double-page spread in its tabloid section, headlined 'Acts in a sex war', in which nine prominent figures who'd seen the play were asked for their views. Here are some of them:

'By linking political correctness with sexual harassment, Mamet trivialises real issues of power and domination. Carol is just an inadequate student seeking revenge against the clever.' (Anne Karpf, writer)

'Even before John put his arm around Carol I was shocked at his arrogant invasion of her verbal space, the way he put words in her mouth. But then the lecturer touches the student. That was mistaken, even if it was done for comfort ... it wasn't just John browbeating and touching Carol, it was an expression of patriarchal and institutional power that got a tragic comeuppance.' (Peter M. Lewis, academic)

'A crude piece of theatre with little drama and zero ambiguity, with the cards grossly stacked against the female character.' (Sarah Dunant, novelist and broadcaster)

'We are forced by this play once again to re-examine our motivations. When we try to help our fellow human beings whose position is much weaker than ours, our own self-esteem may well be enhanced by the virtuous exercise. Are we making sure that on balance we are enhancing theirs?' (Lord Longford, campaigner for penal reform)

For several months after the Royal Court production opened, photographs of Williams and Suchet in *Oleanna* were used as generic illustration for a number of newspaper features about real-life rape and sexual harassment cases, including a *Sunday Times* piece by Christa D'Souza on 17 October 1993 that asked, 'When is a rape not a rape?'

Oleanna on film

In 1994, Mamet directed a film of *Oleanna* from a screenplay whose dialogue is virtually identical to the play's, save for a few additional lines. It stars a bearded William H. Macy, who had played John in the American première of the play, and Debra Eisenstadt, a young actress with pale features and light brown, curly hair.

In order to open out the drama from the confines of a single set and make Carol's and John's conversations less static, Mamet relocates some of the action and introduces several bridging scenes.

After an establishing shot of an elegant, whitewashed college building with a beautiful lawn in the foreground on a sunny day, Carol is seen reaching the head of a queue of male and female students who have come to collect their post from a faculty office.

She retreats to a deserted staircase before opening the letter she has received and absorbing the contents. We then see her in her dorm room, where she rereads the letter, looks anxious, and then grabs her bag and heads out. We may later infer that the letter has come from her parents, perhaps asking how she's getting on, but whoever sent it, it is undoubtedly the catalyst for her going to see John about her grade, apparently on impulse, rather than as part of a pre-planned set-up (see discussion of Carol's note-taking in 'Carol', p. xlviii).

We cut to John's office, where he is in the midst of the play's opening phone call, Carol is sitting opposite his desk, and the dialogue begins as in the play. Instead of the action staying within John's office, however, Mamet keeps Carol and John on the move, as the latter repeatedly tries and fails to leave the building. By the equivalent of page 10 he has packed his briefcase, left and locked his office with Carol following him to a nearby classroom where he has left a thick paperback, *Questions and Answers on Real Estate*.

After Carol says 'It's pathetic, isn't it', both sit down and John begins to tell her about being raised to think himself stupid. He starts to leave the building again (at p. 17) and they continue the conversation in the corridor and at a reception desk, on which someone has left a paper aeroplane that inspires

John to tell his pilot story.

John might now leave, were it not for the intervention of a middle-aged female administrative secretary who hands him a thick bundle of papers and we hear him, off camera, say 'I'm never going to get out of here today'. He then returns to his office to leave the bundle on his desk and is about to lock the door when the third phone call comes through. Carol loiters at the door as John is on the phone and then he sits down, having decided to give Carol more of his time.

By this point it has become clear that Mamet has chosen to sacrifice much of the claustrophobic intensity of the stage production. Instead, he wants to keep *Oleanna* the movie on the move and to use cinema's broader scope to give the audience a greater sense of the two characters' place within the wider college community, hence the shots of students, teachers, administrative staff. The effect, as is often the case with stage-to-screen adaptations, is to show cinemagoers the world of the play that will, of necessity, be left to theatregoers' imagination. For example, when Carol says 'There are *people* out there' who came to the college to be helped, we have a clear image of her fellow students queuing for their post – and perhaps confronting the same intellectual and career anxieties. Yet this broadened canvas will also create problems for the drama.

The pair continue talking in John's office until he offers Carol a cup of tea – the most notable of several additional details within Macy's performance that make John a more sympathetic figure than he was in the Royal Court production (it's impossible to imagine David Suchet offering Lia Williams the same courtesy).

John has to go to a kitchen that is on the far side of the committee room adjacent to his office. This room is a wood-panelled affair with a glass-fronted trophy cabinet and an imposing bust of a Roman emperor (exactly the kind of 'élitist' furnishings that would intimidate someone like Carol). As John boils the kettle Carol's eye is drawn to an inscription that runs along the walls: 'We will be judged by that least involved of magistrates: history' (a rather heavy-handed pointer to the judicial process to come).

John sits with his feet on the committee table as he talks of

the 'Bad Tenure Committee' (adding hubristic physical
disrespect to the verbal slights), then they return to his office.
In her exasperation at John's constant interruptions Carol
accidentally drops and smashes her cup. She goes back into the
conference room to declare 'I'm bad' and both are at the table
in an increasingly dark room (it's now dusk) as she prepares to
make her confession. But John returns to his office to take the
last of Act One's phone calls, so that the physical separation
accentuates the gap between the characters more emphatically
than on stage: Carol in the foreground, alone in the darkened
committee room, John in his brightly lit office, learning of the
surprise party.

After John tells Carol of the surprise party there is a fade
into an interlude showing John in the living room of his large
two-storey home. It is the aftermath of his surprise party and
he's received various presents.

As he goes out to sit on the porch and enjoy a final glass of
champagne, we catch a glimpse of Grace through a window,
her back to the camera. We see rather than imagine what he
goes back to during the interval between Acts One and Two in
the stage production: his sense of 'invulnerable' fulfilment in the
beautiful family home.

Mamet then cuts to John washing his hands in a men's toilet
at the college. Macy has made a costume change very similar
to David Suchet's in the Royal Court production – from smart-
casual attire (sports jacket, check shirt, wool tie) to a business
suit. The action returns to John's office and when we see Carol
the transformation in her appearance is startling.

In Act One she wore a tomboyish outfit of boots, light-blue
trousers, light-grey T-shirt under dark-grey sweater, and she
carried a grey, army-surplus jacket. For Act Two she wears an
ill-fitting man's two-piece grey suit and black waistcoat, white
open-necked shirt, with her curly hair no longer hanging loosely
but scraped back into a ponytail. Her canvas bag has been
replaced by a smart leather document wallet. Her
empowerment is demonstrated by clothes so deliberately
masculine that she might be on her way to a drag party,
masquerading as a corporate lawyer. In the final act she wears
a printed skirt and black T-shirt beneath another ill-fitting male

jacket, and both costume changes make the transformation in her behaviour seem even more radical than on stage (as will an interlude later in the film).

Eisenstadt does little to humanise Carol, giving a performance more strident and less varied than Lia Williams, delivering her lines with almost robotic monotony in generally shrill tones. Macy, too, delivers his lines with much less variation than David Suchet and both actors in the film use the relatively uninflected vocal style that Mamet favours when directing his own work.

The cinematic opening out of the drama resumes at the end of Act Two after John tries to restrain Carol from leaving. She rushes out into the corridor shouting, 'Would somebody help me, please?' We see several middle-aged, earnest-looking figures outside the door to the adjoining room: this must be the tenure committee, about to assess Carol's original complaint.

This is a fascinating change (and perhaps the only one in Carol's favour in the whole film), because now Carol's allegation will be made directly to the people who are about to hear the first complaint. They will have witnessed her distress after the 'attempted rape' and it is therefore easier to understand why the committee might accept her version of events, compared to the 'her word-against his' version implicit in the staging of Act Two.

An interlude between Acts Two and Three shows a dishevelled John in a hotel bedroom. There are room service platters on his bed as he smokes and scribbles notes on to the tenure committee report. Coming after the post-party scene, it completes a vivid picture of John's fall – from dream family home to lonely hotel room.

Then comes the weakest moment in the film, as Mamet pushes Carol's newly acquired militancy to almost caricatured extremes. We see her making multiple photocopies of a statement that reads: 'For sexual misconduct and for injustice to the student body I have come to apologise as I see that I have failed in my responsibilities to the young.' She rubber-stamps each one with what must be the group's emblem.

But why is Carol preparing so many copies of the statement before she even knows if John is willing to sign it, given that he need only sign the original, which she could have copied? Because, I would argue, this scene owes less to Carol's integrity as a character than it does to the expediency of cinematic narrative and the tendency for screen adaptations to render explicit aspects of a story that may safely remain in a theatre audience's imagination.

Carol also asks the male copy-shop assistant if he can make enlargements of a text that we then see stuck up as a poster in a corridor near John's office. It is a student manifesto beginning 'It is the right of all students to be treated with respect' and ending in a call for the university system to undergo overdue reformation.

The posters, printed apologies and group logo may well reflect the activities of student lobbyists on US campuses in the 1990s, but, like the costume changes, they stamp Carol as a stereotypical militant and thus a less interesting character than on the page and in the Royal Court production. Her trip to the copy shop appears to be evidence of a one-woman revolution rather than the concerted student action that would seem credible if we saw even ten seconds of Carol with her group.

Mamet undercuts the dramatically effective ambiguity of John's and Carol's motives and behaviour by fostering confusion in the viewer's mind about what's going on elsewhere on campus. This problem arises because the film repeatedly takes a few steps towards becoming the expanded version of *Oleanna* that I posited on p. lviii, then returns to the intimate stage model. The other students, the tenure committee and Grace remain mute, and we do not see the group at all. As a result, John and Carol are left in a dramatic no-man's-land. They are simultaneously part of a credible university environment and yet strangely secluded from it by Mamet's decision not to alter the two-hander format and write dialogue for the other characters.

The feeling that *Oleanna* is a cruder work on screen than on stage, its ironies more heavily underscored, is compounded by Mamet's use of music. The opening and closing credits run beneath renditions of 'Our College Days', with lyrics by Mamet and piano music by Rebecca Pidgeon, a beautiful but deeply ironic pastiche of some early-twentieth-century college anthem: a hymn to the joys of campus life. When John is at home in the aftermath of the party the soundtrack plays 'Hail the Men of Merit', as a male choir praise the academics 'who have worn the moral crown'.

The film shows us the world of the play with greater breadth and verisimilitude than could ever be achieved in the theatre, and when Mamet confines the action to John's office and the committee room much of the power of the London stage production is preserved. However, the weaknesses outlined above illustrate how the intensity of a claustrophobic, single-set two-hander can be diluted on screen, and how the complex ambiguities of theatre can be over-simplified by the more literal medium of film.

In the screen version, Mamet favours the 'show don't tell' conventions of filmic realism. On stage, our need to imagine the people and places beyond the confines of the set adds yet more ambiguity to the drama, because each member of the audience will have his or her own mental picture of Grace, John's dream home, the tenure committee etc., just as there will be hundreds of different responses to the rights and wrongs of the characters' viewpoints. With the more literal film version, we do not have to exercise our imaginations as strenuously and *Oleanna* is a play that deserves and demands hard work from its audiences.

Further Reading

Books by Mamet

Plays

David Mamet Plays: 1, Methuen, London, 1994; contains *Duck Variations, Sexual Perversity in Chicago, Squirrels, American Buffalo, The Water Engine, Mr Happiness*

David Mamet Plays: 2, Methuen, London, 1996; contains *Reunion, Dark Pony, A Life in the Theatre, The Woods, Lakeboat, Edmond*

David Mamet Plays: 3, Methuen, London, 1996; contains *Glengarry Glen Ross, Prairie du Chien, The Shawl, Speed-the-Plow*

David Mamet Plays: 4, Methuen, London, 2002; contains *Oleanna, The Cryptogram, The Old Neighborhood*

Dramatic Sketches and Monologues, Samuel French, London, 1985

Five Television Plays, Grove, New York, 1990; contains *A Waitress in Yellowstone, Bradford, The Museum of Science and Industry Story, A Wasted Weekend, We Will Take You There*

Short Plays and Monologues, Dramatists Play Service, New York, 1981; contains *All Men Are Whores, The Blue Hour, In Old Vermont, Litko, Prairie du Chien, A Sermon, Shoeshine*

Three Children's Plays, Grove, New York, 1986; contains *The Poet and the Rent, The Frog Prince, The Revenge of the Space Pandas*

Three Jewish Plays, Samuel French, London, 1987; contains *The Disappearance of the Jews, Goldberg Street, The Luftmensch*

Three Plays: Reunion, Dark Pony, The Sanctity of Marriage, Samuel French, London, 1982

Boston Marriage, Methuen, London, 2001

Selected other works
*Three Uses of the Knife: On the Nature and Purpose of
   Drama*, Methuen, London, 2002
A Whore's Profession: Notes and Essays, Faber, London, 1994
True and False: Heresy and Common Sense for the Actor,
   Faber, London, 1998
Writing in Restaurants, Faber, London, 1988

Film and video

Oleanna (1994, dir. David Mamet)
Glengarry Glen Ross (1992, dir. James Foley)
American Buffalo (1996, dir. Michael Corrente)

Oleanna – video recording. The Theatre Museum in Covent
   Garden, London, holds a video recording of the Royal Court
   production, viewable by appointment

Books, essays and articles on David Mamet

C.W.E. Bigsby, 'David Mamet: All True Stories', *Modern
   American Drama*, Cambridge University Press, Cambridge,
   2000
Christopher Hudgins and Leslie Kane (eds), *Gender and Genre:
   Essays on David Mamet*, Palgrave, New York, 2001
Leslie Kane (ed.), *Weasels and Wisemen: Ethics and Ethnicity
   in the Work of David Mamet*, St Martin's Press, New York,
   1999
Leslie Kane (ed.), *David Mamet in Conversation*, University of
   Michigan Press, Ann Arbor, 2001. Invaluable collection of
   lengthy press and television interviews with Mamet, including
   the *South Bank Show*, *Charlie Rose Show* and *Playboy*
   conversations quoted
Matthew Charles Roudane, 'Theatrician of the Ethical? The
   Plays of David Mamet', in *American Drama Since 1960*,
   Twayne, New York, 1996
London Theatre Record, vol. XIII, no. 13, 1993, pp. 740–7.
   Contains all national newspaper reviews of the Royal Court
   production of *Oleanna*

'Acts in a sex war', *Guardian*, 7 July 1993. Selection of
impassioned male and female reactions to the Royal Court
production of *Oleanna*

Books on political correctness and sexual harassment

Berman, Paul (ed.), *Debating PC – The Controversy Over
Political Correctness on College Campuses*, Laurel, New
York, 1992

Several books deal extensively with the Anita Hills *v.* Clarence
Thomas case, including:

Jane Flax, *The American Dream in Black and White: The
Clarence Thomas Hearings,* Cornell University Press, Ithaca,
1999
Jane Mayer and Jill Abramson, *Strange Justice: The Selling of
Clarence Thomas*, Houghton Mifflin, New York, 1994
Andrew Peyton Thomas, *Clarence Thomas: A Biography*,
Encounter Books, 2002

Relevant works by other writers

Edward Albee, *Marriage Play*, Dramatists Play Service, New
York, 1995
J.M. Coetzee, *Disgrace*, Secker & Warburg, London, 1999
David Hare, *Skylight*, Faber, London, 1995
Arthur Miller, *The Crucible*, Penguin, London, 1968
Philip Roth, *The Human Stain*, Jonathan Cape, London, 2000

OLEANNA

This play is dedicated to the memory of
Michael Merrit

Oleanna was first performed in the United States, at the American Repertory Theatre, Massachusetts, on 1 May 1992.

Oleanna was first performed in the United Kingdom at the Royal Court Theatre, London, on 24 June 1993. The cast was as follows:

JOHN   David Suchet
CAROL   Lia Williams

Directed by Harold Pinter
Designed by Eileen Diss
Lighting by Gerry Jenkinson
Sound by Lorna Earl

ONE

□□□

JOHN *is talking on the phone.* CAROL *is seated across the desk from him.*

JOHN (*on phone*): And what about the land. (*Pause*) The land. And what about the land? (*Pause*) What about it? (*Pause*) No. I don't understand. Well, yes, I'm I'm . . . no, I'm *sure* it's signif . . . I'm sure it's significant. (*Pause*) Because it's significant to mmmmmm . . . did you call Jerry? (*Pause*) Because . . . no, no, no, no, no. What did they say . . . ? Did you speak to the *real* estate . . . where *is* she . . . ? Well, well, all right. Where are her notes? Where are the notes we took with her. (*Pause*) I thought you were? No. No, I'm sorry, I didn't mean that, I just thought that I saw you, when we were there . . . what . . . ? I thought I saw you with a *pencil*. WHY NOW? is what I'm say . . . well, that's why I say "call Jerry." Well, I can't right now, be . . . no, I *didn't* schedule any . . . Grace: I *didn't* . . . I'm well aware . . . Look: Look. Did you call Jerry? Will you call Jerry . . . ? Because I can't now. I'll be there, I'm sure I'll be there in fifteen, in twenty. I intend to. No, we aren't *going* to lose the, we aren't *going* to lose the house. Look: Look, I'm not minimizing it. The "easement." Did she say "easement"? (*Pause*) What did she *say; is* it a "term of art," are we *bound* by it . . . I'm sorry . . . (*Pause*) are: we: yes. *Bound* by . . . Look: (*He checks his watch.*) before the other side *goes home,* all right? "a term of art." Because: that's right (*Pause*) The yard for the boy. Well, that's the whole . . . Look: I'm going to meet you there . . . (*He checks his watch.*) Is the realtor there? All right, tell her to show you the basement again. Look at the *this* because . . . Bec . . . I'm leaving in, I'm leaving in ten or fifteen . . . Yes. No, no, I'll meet you at the new . . . That's a good. If he thinks it's necc . . . you tell Jerry to meet . . . All right? We *aren't* going to lose the deposit. All right? I'm sure it's going to be . . . (*Pause*) I hope so. (*Pause*) I love you, too. (*Pause*) I love you, too. As soon as . . . I will.

(*He hangs up.*) (*He bends over the desk and makes a note.*) (*He looks up.*) (*To* CAROL:) I'm sorry . . .

CAROL: (*Pause*) What is a "term of art"?

JOHN: (*Pause*) I'm sorry . . . ?

CAROL: (*Pause*) What is a "term of art"?

JOHN: Is that what you want to talk about?

CAROL: . . . to talk about . . . ?

JOHN: Let's take the mysticism out of it, shall we? Carol? (*Pause*) Don't you think? I'll tell you: when you have some "thing." Which must be broached. (*Pause*) Don't you think . . . ? (*Pause*)

CAROL: . . . don't I think . . . ?

JOHN: Mmm?

CAROL: . . . did I . . . ?

JOHN: . . . what?

CAROL: Did . . . did I . . . did I say something wr . . .

JOHN: (*Pause*) No. I'm sorry. No. You're right. I'm very sorry. I'm somewhat rushed. As you see. I'm sorry. You're right. (*Pause*) What is a "term of art"? It seems to mean a *term,* which has come, through its use, to mean something *more specific* than the words would, to someone *not acquainted* with them . . . indicate. That, I believe, is what a "term of art," would mean. (*Pause*)

CAROL: You don't know what it means . . . ?

JOHN: I'm not sure that I know what it means. It's one of those things, perhaps you've had them, that,

you look them up, or have someone explain
them to you, and you say "aha," and, you immediately *forget* what . . .

CAROL: You don't do that.

JOHN: . . . I . . . ?

CAROL: You don't do . . .

JOHN: . . . I don't, what . . . ?

CAROL: . . . for . . .

JOHN: . . . I don't for . . .

CAROL: . . . no . . .

JOHN: . . . forget things? Everybody does that.

CAROL: No, they don't.

JOHN: They don't . . .

CAROL: No.

JOHN: (*Pause*) No. Everybody does that.

CAROL: Why would they do that . . . ?

JOHN: Because. I don't know. Because it doesn't interest them.

CAROL: No.

JOHN: I think so, though. (*Pause*) I'm sorry that I was distracted.

CAROL: You don't have to say that to me.

JOHN: You paid me the compliment, or the "obeisance"—all right—of coming in here . . . All right. *Carol*. I find that I am at a *standstill*. I find that I . . .

CAROL: . . . what . . .

JOHN: . . . one moment. In regard to your . . . to your . . .

CAROL: Oh, oh. You're buying a new house!

JOHN: No, let's get on with it.

CAROL: "get on"? (*Pause*)

JOHN: I know how . . . *believe* me. I know how . . . potentially *humiliating* these . . . I have no desire to . . . I have no desire other than to help you. But: (*He picks up some papers on his desk.*) I won't even say "but." I'll say that as I go back over the . . .

CAROL: I'm just, I'm just trying to . . .

JOHN: . . . no, it will not do.

CAROL: . . . what? What will . . . ?

JOHN: No. I see, I see what you, it . . . (*He gestures to the papers.*) but your work . . .

CAROL: I'm just: I sit in class I . . . (*She holds up her notebook.*) I take notes . . .

JOHN (*simultaneously with* "notes"): Yes. I understand. What I am trying to *tell* you is that some, some basic . . .

CAROL: . . . I . . .

JOHN: . . . one moment: some basic missed communi . . .

CAROL: I'm doing what I'm told. I bought your book, I read your . . .

JOHN: No, I'm sure you . . .

CAROL: No, no, no. I'm doing what I'm told. It's *difficult* for me. It's *difficult* . . .

JOHN: . . . but . . .

CAROL: I don't . . . lots of the *language* . . .

JOHN: . . . please . . .

CAROL: The *language*, the "things" that you say . . .

JOHN: I'm sorry. No. I don't think that that's true.

CAROL: It *is* true. I . . .

JOHN: I think . . .

CAROL: It *is* true.

JOHN: . . . I . . .

CAROL: Why would I . . . ?

JOHN: I'll tell you why: you're an incredibly bright girl.

CAROL: . . . I . . .

JOHN: You're an incredibly . . . you have no problem with the . . . Who's kidding who?

CAROL: . . . I . . .

JOHN: No. No. I'll tell you why. I'll tell . . . . I think you're *angry*, I . . .

CAROL: . . . why would I . . .

JOHN: . . . wait one moment. I . . .

CAROL: It *is* true. I have *problems* . . .

JOHN: . . . every . . .

CAROL: . . . I come from a different *social* . . .

JOHN: . . . ev . . .

CAROL: a different economic . . .

JOHN: . . . Look:

CAROL: No. I: when I *came* to this school:

JOHN: Yes. Quite . . . (*Pause*)

CAROL: . . . does that mean nothing . . . ?

JOHN: . . . but look: look . . .

CAROL: . . . I . . .

JOHN: (*Picks up paper.*) Here: Please: Sit down. (*Pause*) Sit down. (*Reads from her paper.*) "I think that the ideas contained in this work express the author's feelings in a way that he intended, based on his results." What can that mean? Do you see? What . . .

CAROL: I, the best that I . . .

JOHN: I'm saying, that perhaps this course . . .

CAROL: No, no, no, you can't, you can't . . . I have to . . .

JOHN: . . . how . . .

CAROL: . . . I have to pass it . . .

JOHN: Carol, I:

CAROL: I *have* to pass this course, I . . .

JOHN: Well.

CAROL: . . . don't you . . .

JOHN: Either the . . .

CAROL: . . . I . . .

JOHN: . . . either the, I . . . either the *criteria* for judging progress in the class are . . .

CAROL: No, no, no, no, I have to pass it.

JOHN: Now, look: I'm a human being, I . . .

CAROL: I did what you told me. I did, I did everything that, I read your *book,* you told me to buy your book and read it. Everything you *say* I . . . (*She gestures to her notebook.*) (*The phone rings.*) I do. . . . Ev . . .

JOHN: . . . look:

CAROL: . . . everything I'm told . . .

JOHN: Look. Look. I'm not your *father.* (*Pause*)

CAROL: What?

JOHN: I'm.

CAROL: Did I say you were my father?

JOHN: . . . no . . .

CAROL: Why did you say that . . . ?

JOHN: I . . .

CAROL: . . . why . . . ?

JOHN: . . . in class I . . . (*He picks up the phone.*) (*Into phone:*) Hello. I can't talk now. Jerry? Yes? I underst . . . I can't talk now. I know . . . I know . . . Jerry. I can't *talk* now. Yes, I. Call me back in . . . Thank you. (*He hangs up.*) (*To* CAROL:) What do you want me to do? We are two people, all right? Both of whom have subscribed to . . .

CAROL: No, no . . .

JOHN: . . . certain arbitrary . . .

CAROL: No. You have to help me.

JOHN: Certain institutional . . . you tell me what you want me to do. . . . You tell me what you want me to . . .

CAROL: How can I go back and tell them the *grades* that I . . .

JOHN: . . . what can I do . . . ?

CAROL: *Teach* me. *Teach* me.

JOHN: . . . I'm trying to teach you.

CAROL: I read your book. I read it. I don't under . . .

JOHN: . . . you don't understand it.

CAROL: No.

JOHN: Well, perhaps it's not well *written* . . .

CAROL (*simultaneously with* "written"): No. No. No. I want to *understand* it.

JOHN: What don't you understand? (*Pause*)

CAROL: *Any* of it. What you're trying to say. When you talk about . . .

JOHN: . . . yes . . . ? (*She consults her notes.*)

CAROL: "Virtual warehousing of the young" . . .

JOHN: "Virtual warehousing of the young." If we artificially prolong adolescence . . .

CAROL: . . . and about "The Curse of Modern Education."

JOHN: . . . well . . .

CAROL: I don't . . .

JOHN: Look. It's just a *course,* it's just a *book,* it's just a . . .

CAROL: No. No. There are *people* out there. People who came *here.* To know something they didn't *know.* Who *came* here. To be *helped.* To be *helped.* So someone would *help* them. To *do* something. To *know* something. To get, what do they say? "To get on in the world." How can I do that if I don't, if I fail? But I don't *understand.* I don't *understand.* I don't understand what anything means . . . and I walk around. From morning 'til night: with this one thought in my head. I'm *stupid.*

JOHN: No one thinks you're stupid.

CAROL: No? What am I . . . ?

JOHN: I . . .

CAROL: . . . what am I, then?

JOHN: I think you're angry. Many people are. I have a *telephone* call that I have to make. And an *ap-*

pointment, which is rather *pressing;* though I sympathize with your concerns, and though I wish I had the time, this was not a previously scheduled meeting and I . . .

CAROL: . . . you think I'm nothing . . .

JOHN: . . . have an appointment with a *realtor,* and with my wife and . . .

CAROL: You think that I'm stupid.

JOHN: No. I certainly don't.

CAROL: You said it.

JOHN: No. I did not.

CAROL: You did.

JOHN: When?

CAROL: . . . you . . .

JOHN: No. I never did, or never would say that to a student, and . . .

CAROL: You said, "What can that mean?" (*Pause*) "What can that mean?" . . . (*Pause*)

JOHN: . . . and what did that mean to you . . . ?

CAROL: That meant I'm stupid. And I'll never learn. That's what that meant. And you're right.

JOHN: . . . I . . .

CAROL: But then. But then, what am I doing here . . . ?

JOHN: . . . if you thought that I . . .

CAROL: . . . when nobody wants me, and . . .

JOHN: . . . if you interpreted . . .

CAROL: Nobody *tells* me anything. And I *sit* there . . . in the *corner*. In the *back*. And everybody's talking about "this" all the time. And "concepts," and "precepts" and, and, and, and, and, WHAT IN THE WORLD ARE YOU *TALKING* ABOUT? And I read your book. And they said, "Fine, go in that class." Because you talked about responsibility to the young. I DON'T KNOW WHAT IT MEANS AND I'M *FAILING* . . .

JOHN: May . . .

CAROL: No, you're right. "Oh, hell." I failed. Flunk me out of it. It's garbage. Everything I do. "The ideas contained in this work express the author's feelings." That's right. That's right. I know I'm stupid. I know what I am. (*Pause*) I know what

I am, Professor. You don't have to tell me. (*Pause*) It's pathetic. Isn't it?

JOHN: . . . Aha . . . (*Pause*) Sit down. Sit down. Please. (*Pause*) Please sit down.

CAROL: Why?

JOHN: I want to talk to you.

CAROL: Why?

JOHN: Just sit down. (*Pause*) Please. Sit down. Will you, please . . . ? (*Pause. She does so.*) Thank you.

CAROL: What?

JOHN: I want to tell you something.

CAROL: (*Pause*) What?

JOHN: Well, I know what you're talking about.

CAROL: No. You don't.

JOHN: I think I do. (*Pause*)

CAROL: How can you?

JOHN: I'll tell you a story about myself. (*Pause*) Do you mind? (*Pause*) I was raised to think myself stupid. That's what I want to tell you. (*Pause*)

CAROL: What do you mean?

JOHN: Just what I said. I was brought up, and my earliest, and most persistent memories are of being told that I was stupid. "You have such *intelligence*. Why must you behave so *stupidly*?" Or, "Can't you *understand*? Can't you *understand*?" And I could *not* understand. I could *not* understand.

CAROL: What?

JOHN: The simplest problem. Was beyond me. It was a mystery.

CAROL: What was a mystery?

JOHN: How people learn. How *I* could learn. Which is what I've been speaking of in class. And of *course* you can't hear it. Carol. Of *course* you can't. (*Pause*) I used to speak of "real people," and wonder what the *real* people did. The *real* people. Who were they? *They* were the people other than myself. The *good* people. The *capable* people. The people who could do the things, *I* could not do: learn, study, retain . . . all that *garbage*—which is what I have been talking of in class, and that's *exactly* what I have been talking of—If you are told . . . . Listen to this. If the young child is told he cannot understand. Then he takes it as a *description* of himself. What am I? I am *that which can not understand.* And I saw you

out there, when we were speaking of the concepts of . . .

CAROL: I can't understand any of them.

JOHN: Well, then, that's *my* fault. That's not your
fault. And that is not verbiage. That's what I
firmly hold to be the truth. And I am sorry, and
I owe you an apology.

CAROL: Why?

JOHN: And I suppose that I have had some *things* on
my mind. . . . We're buying a *house*, and . . .

CAROL: People said that you were stupid . . . ?

JOHN: Yes.

CAROL: When?

JOHN: I'll tell you when. Through my life. In my
childhood; and, perhaps, they stopped. But I
heard them continue.

CAROL: And what did they say?

JOHN: They said I was incompetent. Do you see? And
when I'm tested the, the, the *feelings* of my youth
about the *very subject of learning* come up. And I
. . . I become, I feel "unworthy," and "unpre-
pared." . . .

CAROL: . . . yes.

JOHN: . . . eh?

CAROL: . . . yes.

JOHN: And I feel that I must fail. (*Pause*)

CAROL: . . . but then you *do* fail. (*Pause*) You have to. (*Pause*) Don't you?

JOHN: A *pilot*. Flying a plane. The pilot is flying the plane. He thinks: Oh, my *God*, my mind's been drifting! Oh, my God! What kind of a cursed imbecile am I, that I, with this so precious cargo of *Life* in my charge, would allow my attention to wander. Why was I born? How deluded are those who put their trust in me, . . . et cetera, so on, and he crashes the plane.

CAROL: (*Pause*) He could just . . .

JOHN: That's right.

CAROL: He could say:

JOHN: My attention *wandered* for a moment . . .

CAROL: . . . uh huh . . .

JOHN: I had a *thought* I did not like . . . but now:

CAROL: . . . but now it's . . .

JOHN: That's what I'm telling you. It's time to put my attention . . . see: it is not: this is what I learned. It is Not Magic. Yes. Yes. *You.* You are going to be frightened. When faced with what may or may not be but which you are going to perceive as a test. You will become frightened. And you will say: "I am incapable of . . ." and everything *in* you will think these two things. "I must. But I can't." And you will think: Why was I born to be the laughingstock of a world in which everyone is better than I? In which I am entitled to nothing. Where I can not learn.

(*Pause*)

CAROL: Is that . . . (*Pause*) Is that what I have . . . ?

JOHN: Well. I don't know if I'd put it that way. Listen: I'm talking to you as I'd talk to my son. Because that's what I'd like him to have that I never had. I'm talking to you the way I wish that someone had talked to me. I don't know how to do it, other than to be *personal*, . . . but . . .

CAROL: Why would you want to be personal with me?

JOHN: Well, you see? That's what I'm saying. We can only interpret the behavior of others through the screen we . . . (*The phone rings.*) Through . . . (*To phone:*) Hello . . . ? (*To* CAROL:) Through the

screen we create. (*To phone:*) Hello. (*To* CAROL:)
Excuse me a moment. (*To phone:*) Hello? No, I
can't talk nnn . . . I know I did. In a few . . . I'm
. . . is he coming to the . . . yes. I talked to him.
We'll meet you at the No, because I'm with a
student. It's going to be fff . . . This is important,
too. I'm with a *student,* Jerry's going to . . .
Listen: the sooner I get off, the sooner I'll be
down, all right. I love you. Listen, listen, I said
"I love you," it's going to work *out* with the,
because I feel that it is, I'll be right down. All
right? Well, then it's going to take as long as it
takes. (*He hangs up.*) (*To* CAROL:) I'm sorry.

CAROL: What was that?

JOHN: There are some problems, as there usually are,
about the final agreements for the new house.

CAROL: You're buying a new house.

JOHN: That's right.

CAROL: Because of your promotion.

JOHN: Well, I suppose that that's right.

CAROL: Why did you stay here with me?

JOHN: Stay here.

CAROL: Yes. When you should have gone.

JOHN: Because I like you.

CAROL: You like me.

JOHN: Yes.

CAROL: Why?

JOHN: Why? Well? Perhaps we're similar. (*Pause*) Yes. (*Pause*)

CAROL: You said "everyone has problems."

JOHN: Everyone has problems.

CAROL: Do they?

JOHN: Certainly.

CAROL: You do?

JOHN: Yes.

CAROL: What are they?

JOHN: Well. (*Pause*) Well, you're perfectly right. (*Pause*) If we're going to take off the Artificial *Stricture*, of "Teacher," and "Student," why should *my* problems be any more a mystery than your own? Of *course* I have problems. As you saw.

CAROL: . . . with what?

JOHN: With my *wife* . . . with *work* . . .

CAROL: With work?

JOHN: Yes. And, and, perhaps my problems are, do you see? *Similar* to yours.

CAROL: Would you tell me?

JOHN: All right. (*Pause*) I came *late* to teaching. And I found it Artificial. The notion of "I know and you do not"; and I saw an *exploitation* in the education process. I told you. I hated school, I hated teachers. I hated everyone who was in the position of a "boss" because I *knew*—I didn't *think*, mind you, I *knew* I was going to fail. Because I was a fuckup. I was just no goddamned good. When I . . . late in life . . . (*Pause*) When I *got out from under* . . . when I worked my way out of the need to fail. When I . . .

CAROL: How do you do that? (*Pause*)

JOHN: You have to look at what you are, and what you feel, and how you act. And, finally, you have to look at how you act. And say: If that's what I *did*, that must be how I think of myself.

CAROL: I don't understand.

JOHN: If I fail all the time, it must be that I think of myself as a failure. If I do not want to think of myself as a failure, perhaps I should begin by *succeeding* now and again. Look. The tests, you see, which you encounter, in school, in college, in life, were designed, in the most part, for idiots. *By* idiots. There is no need to fail at them. They are not a test of your worth. They are a test of your ability to retain and spout back misinformation. Of *course* you fail them. They're *nonsense*. And I . . .

CAROL: . . . no . . .

JOHN: Yes. They're *garbage*. They're a *joke*. Look at me. Look at me. The Tenure Committee. The Tenure Committee. Come to judge me. The Bad Tenure Committee.

The "Test." Do you see? They put me to the test. Why, they had people voting on me I wouldn't employ to wax my car. And yet, I go before the Great Tenure Committee, and I have an urge, to *vomit,* to, to, to puke my *badness* on the table, to show them: "I'm no good. Why would you pick *me*?"

CAROL: They granted you tenure.

JOHN: Oh no, they announced it, but they haven't *signed*. Do you see? "At any moment . . ."

CAROL: . . . mmm . . .

JOHN: "They might not *sign*" . . . I might not . . . the *house* might not go through . . . Eh? Eh? They'll find out my "dark secret." (*Pause*)

CAROL: . . . what is it . . . ?

JOHN: There *isn't* one. But *they* will find an index of my badness . . .

CAROL: Index?

JOHN: A ". . . pointer." A "Pointer." You see? Do you see? I *understand* you. I. Know. That. Feeling. Am I entitled to my job, and my nice *home*, and my *wife*, and my *family*, and so on. This is what I'm saying: That theory of education which, that *theory:*

CAROL: I . . . I . . . (*Pause*)

JOHN: What?

CAROL: I . . .

JOHN: What?

CAROL: I want to know about my grade. (*Long pause*)

JOHN: Of course you do.

CAROL: Is that bad?

JOHN: No.

CAROL: Is it bad that I asked you that?

JOHN: No.

CAROL: Did I upset you?

JOHN: No. And I apologize. Of *course* you want to know about your grade. And, of course, you can't concentrate on anyth . . . (*The telephone starts to ring.*) Wait a moment.

CAROL: I should go.

JOHN: I'll make you a deal.

CAROL: No, you have to . . .

JOHN: Let it ring. I'll make you a deal. You stay here. We'll start the whole course over. I'm going to say it was not you, it was I who was not paying attention. We'll start the whole course over. Your grade is an "A." Your final grade is an "A." (*The phone stops ringing.*)

CAROL: But the class is only half over . . .

JOHN (*simultaneously with* "over"): Your grade for the whole term is an "A." If you will come back and meet with me. A few more times. Your grade's an "A." Forget about the paper. You didn't like it, you didn't like writing it. It's not important.

What's important is that I awake your interest, if I can, and that I answer your questions. Let's start over. (*Pause*)

CAROL: Over. With what?

JOHN: Say this is the beginning.

CAROL: The beginning.

JOHN: Yes.

CAROL: Of what?

JOHN: Of the class.

CAROL: But we can't start over.

JOHN: I say we can. (*Pause*) I say we can.

CAROL: But I don't believe it.

JOHN: Yes, I know that. But it's true. What is The Class but you and me? (*Pause*)

CAROL: There are rules.

JOHN: Well. We'll break them.

CAROL: How can we?

JOHN: We won't tell anybody.

CAROL: Is that all right?

JOHN: I say that it's fine.

CAROL: Why would you do this for me?

JOHN: I like you. Is that so difficult for you to . . .

CAROL: Um . . .

JOHN: There's no one here but you and me. (*Pause*)

CAROL: All right. I did not understand. When you referred . . .

JOHN: All right, yes?

CAROL: When you referred to hazing.

JOHN: Hazing.

CAROL: You wrote, in your book. About the comparative . . . the comparative . . . (*She checks her notes.*)

JOHN: Are you checking your notes . . . ?

CAROL: Yes.

JOHN: Tell me in your own . . .

CAROL: I want to make sure that I have it right.

JOHN: No. Of course. You want to be exact.

CAROL: I want to know everything that went on.

JOHN: . . . that's good.

CAROL: . . . so I . . .

JOHN: That's very good. But I was suggesting, many times, that that which we wish to retain is retained oftentimes, I think, *better* with less expenditure of effort.

CAROL: (*Of notes*) Here it is: you wrote of *hazing*.

JOHN: . . . that's correct. Now: I said "hazing." It means ritualized annoyance. We shove this book at you, we say read it. Now, you say you've read it? I think that you're *lying*. I'll *grill* you, and when I find you've lied, you'll be disgraced, and your life will be ruined. It's a sick game. Why do we do it? Does it educate? In no sense. Well, then, what is higher education? It is something-other-than-useful.

CAROL: What is "something-other-than-useful?"

JOHN: It has become a ritual, it has become an article of faith. That all must be subjected to, or to put it differently, that all are entitled to Higher Education. And my point . . .

CAROL: You disagree with that?

JOHN: Well, let's address that. What do you think?

CAROL: I don't know.

JOHN: What do you think, though? (*Pause*)

CAROL: I don't know.

JOHN: I spoke of it in class. Do you remember my example?

CAROL: Justice.

JOHN: Yes. Can you repeat it to me? (*She looks down at her notebook.*) Without your notes? I ask you as a favor to me, so that I can see if my idea was interesting.

CAROL: You said "justice" . . .

JOHN: Yes?

CAROL: . . . that all are entitled . . . (*Pause*) I . . . I . . . I . . .

JOHN: Yes. To a speedy trial. To a fair trial. But they needn't be given a trial *at all* unless they stand accused. Eh? Justice is their right, should they choose to avail themselves of it, they should have a fair trial. It does not follow, of necessity, a person's life is incomplete without a trial in it. Do you see?

My point is a confusion between equity and *utility* arose. So we confound the *usefulness* of higher education with our, granted, right to equal access to the same. We, in effect, create a *prejudice* toward it, completely independent of . . .

CAROL: . . . that it is prejudice that we should go to school?

JOHN: Exactly. (*Pause*)

CAROL: How can you say that? How . . .

JOHN: Good. Good. *Good*. That's right! Speak up! What is a prejudice? An unreasoned belief. We are all subject to it. None of us is not. When it is threatened, or opposed, we feel anger, and feel, do we not? As you do now. Do you not? Good.

CAROL: . . . but how can you . . .

JOHN: . . . let us examine. Good.

CAROL: How . . .

JOHN: Good. Good. When . . .

CAROL: I'M SPEAKING . . . (*Pause*)

JOHN: I'm sorry.

CAROL: How can you . . .

JOHN: . . . I beg your pardon.

CAROL: That's all right.

JOHN: I beg your pardon.

CAROL: That's all right.

JOHN: I'm sorry I interrupted you.

CAROL: That's all right.

JOHN: You were saying?

CAROL: I was saying . . . I was saying . . . (*She checks her notes.*) How can you say in a class. Say in a college class, that college education is prejudice?

JOHN: I said that our predilection for it . . .

CAROL: Predilection . . .

JOHN: . . . you know what that means.

CAROL: Does it mean "liking"?

JOHN: Yes.

CAROL: But how can you say that? That College . . .

JOHN: . . . that's my *job*, don't you know.

CAROL: What is?

JOHN: To provoke you.

CAROL: No.

JOHN: Oh. Yes, though.

CAROL: To provoke me?

JOHN: That's right.

CAROL: To make me mad?

JOHN: That's right. To force you . . .

CAROL: . . . to make me mad is your job?

JOHN: To force you to . . . listen: (*Pause*) Ah. (*Pause*) When I was young somebody told me, are you ready, the rich copulate less often than the poor. But when they do, they take more of their clothes off. Years. Years, mind you, I would compare experiences of my own to this dictum, saying, aha, this fits the norm, or ah, this is a variation from it. What did it mean? Nothing. It was some jerk thing, some school kid told me that took up room inside my head. (*Pause*)

Somebody told *you,* and you hold it as an article of faith, that higher education is an unassailable good. This notion is so dear to you that when I question it you become angry. Good. Good, I say. Are not those the very things which we should question? I say college education, since the war, has become so a matter of course, and such a fashionable necessity, for those either of or aspiring *to* to the new vast middle class, that we *espouse* it, as a matter of right, and have ceased to ask, "What is it good for?" (*Pause*)

What might be some reasons for pursuit of higher education?
One: A love of learning.
Two: The wish for mastery of a skill.
Three: For economic betterment.
(*Stops. Makes a note.*)

CAROL: I'm keeping you.

JOHN: One moment. I have to make a note . . .

CAROL: It's something that I said?

JOHN: No, we're buying a house.

CAROL: You're buying the new house.

JOHN: To go with the tenure. That's right. Nice *house,* close to the *private school* . . . (*He continues making his note.*) . . . We were talking of economic *betterment* (CAROL *writes in her notebook.*) . . . I was thinking of the School Tax. (*He contin-*

ues writing.) (*To himself:*) . . . *where is it written* that I have to send my child to public school. . . . Is it a law that I have to improve the City Schools at the expense of my own interest? And, is this not simply *The White Man's Burden?* Good. And (*Looks up to* CAROL) . . . does this interest you?

CAROL: No. I'm taking notes . . .

JOHN: You don't have to take notes, you know, you can just listen.

CAROL: I want to make sure I remember it. (*Pause*)

JOHN: I'm not lecturing you, I'm just trying to tell you some things I think.

CAROL: What do you think?

JOHN: Should all kids go to college? *Why* . . .

CAROL: (*Pause*) To learn.

JOHN: But if he does not learn.

CAROL: If the child does not learn?

JOHN: Then why is he in college? Because he was told it was his "right"?

CAROL: Some might find college instructive.

JOHN: I would hope so.

CAROL: But how do they feel? Being told they are wasting their time?

JOHN: I don't think I'm telling them that.

CAROL: You said that education was "prolonged and systematic hazing."

JOHN: Yes. It can be so.

CAROL: . . . if education is so *bad*, why do you do it?

JOHN: I do it because I love it. (*Pause*) Let's . . . . I suggest you look at the demographics, wage-earning capacity, college- and non-college-educated men and women, 1855 to 1980, and let's see if we can wring some worth from the statistics. Eh? And . . .

CAROL: No.

JOHN: What?

CAROL: I can't understand them.

JOHN: . . . you . . . ?

CAROL: . . . the "charts." The *Concepts,* the . . .

JOHN: "Charts" are simply . . .

CAROL: When I leave here . . .

JOHN: Charts, do you see . . .

CAROL: No, I can't . . .

JOHN: You can, though.

CAROL: NO, NO—I DON'T UNDERSTAND.
DO YOU SEE??? I DON'T *UNDER-
STAND* . . .

JOHN: What?

CAROL: *Any* of it. *Any* of it. I'm *smiling* in class, I'm
smiling, the whole time. What are you *talking*
about? What is everyone *talking* about? I don't
understand. I don't know what it *means.* I don't
know what it means to *be* here . . . you tell me
I'm intelligent, and then you tell me I should not
be *here,* what do you *want* with me? What does
it *mean?* Who should I *listen* to . . . I . . .
    (*He goes over to her and puts his arm around her
    shoulder.*)
    NO! (*She walks away from him.*)

JOHN: Sshhhh.

CAROL: No, I don't under . . .

JOHN: Sshhhhh.

CAROL: I don't know what you're *saying* . . .

JOHN: Sshhhhh. It's all right.

CAROL: . . . I have no . . .

JOHN: Sshhhhh. Sshhhhh. Let it go a moment. (*Pause*) Sshhhhh . . . let it go. (*Pause*) Just let it go. (*Pause*) Just let it go. It's all right. (*Pause*) Sshhhhh. (*Pause*) I understand . . . (*Pause*) What do you feel?

CAROL: I feel bad.

JOHN: I know. It's all right.

CAROL: I . . . (*Pause*)

JOHN: What?

CAROL: I . . .

JOHN: What? Tell me.

CAROL: I don't understand you.

JOHN: I know. It's all right.

CAROL: I . . .

JOHN: What? (*Pause*) What? *Tell* me.

CAROL: I can't tell you.

JOHN: No, you must.

CAROL: I can't.

JOHN: No. Tell me. (*Pause*)

CAROL: I'm bad. (*Pause*) Oh, God. (*Pause*)

JOHN: It's all right.

CAROL: I'm . . .

JOHN: It's all right.

CAROL: I can't talk about this.

JOHN: It's all right. Tell me.

CAROL: Why do you want to know this?

JOHN: I don't want to know. I want to know whatever you . . .

CAROL: I always . . .

JOHN: . . . good . . .

CAROL: I always . . . all my life . . . I have never told anyone this . . .

JOHN: Yes. Go on. (*Pause*) Go on.

CAROL: All of my life . . . (*The phone rings.*) (*Pause.* JOHN *goes to the phone and picks it up.*)

JOHN (*into phone*): I can't talk now. (*Pause*) What? (*Pause*) Hmm. (*Pause*) All right, I . . . I. Can't.

Talk. Now. No, no, no, I *Know* I did, but
. . . . What? Hello. What? She *what?* She *can't,*
she said the agreement is void? How, how is the
agreement *void? That's Our House.*

I have the *paper;* when we come down, next
week, with the payment, and the paper, that
house is . . . wait, wait, wait, wait, wait, wait,
wait: Did Jerry . . . is Jerry there? (*Pause*) Is *she*
there . . . ? Does she have a *lawyer . . . ?* How the
hell, how the *Hell.* That is . . . it's a question, you
said, of the *easement.* I don't underst . . . it's not
the *whole agreement.* It's just the *easement,* why
would she? Put, put, put, *Jerry* on. (*Pause*) Jer,
Jerry: What the *Hell* . . . that's my *house.* That's
. . . Well, I'm, no, no, no, I'm *not* coming ddd
. . . List, *Listen, screw* her. You *tell* her. You,
listen: I want you to take *Grace,* you take Grace,
and get out of that house. You *leave* her there.
Her and her lawyer, and you *tell* them, we'll see
them in court next . . . no. No. Leave her there,
leave her to *stew* in it: You tell her, we're *getting*
that house, and we are going to . . . No. I'm *not*
coming down. I'll be damned if I'll sit in the
same rrr . . . the next, you tell her the next time
I *see* her is in court . . . I . . . (*Pause*) What? (*Pause*)
What? I don't understand. (*Pause*) Well, what
about the house? (*Pause*) There isn't any problem
with the hhh . . . (*Pause*) No, no, no, that's all
right. All ri . . . All right . . . (*Pause*) Of course.
Tha . . . Thank you. No, I will. Right away. (*He
hangs up.*) (*Pause*)

CAROL: What is it? (*Pause*)

JOHN: It's a surprise party.

CAROL: It is.

JOHN: Yes.

CAROL: A party for you.

JOHN: Yes.

CAROL: Is it your birthday?

JOHN: No.

CAROL: What is it?

JOHN: The tenure announcement.

CAROL: The tenure announcement.

JOHN: They're throwing a party for us in our new house.

CAROL: Your new house.

JOHN: The house that we're buying.

CAROL: You have to go.

JOHN: It seems that I do.

CAROL: (*Pause*) They're proud of you.

JOHN: Well, there are those who would say it's a form
    of aggression.

CAROL: What is?

JOHN: A surprise.

TWO

□□□

JOHN and CAROL seated across the desk from each other.

JOHN: You see, (*pause*) I love to teach. And flatter myself I am *skilled* at it. And I love the, the aspect of *performance*. I think I must confess that.

When I found I loved to teach I swore that I would not become that cold, rigid automaton of an instructor which I had encountered as a child.

Now, I was not unconscious that it was given me to err upon the other side. And, so, I asked and *ask* myself if I engaged in heterodoxy, I will not say "gratuitously" for I do not care to posit orthodoxy as a given good—but, "to the detriment of, of my students." (*Pause*)

As I said. When the possibility of tenure opened, and, of course, I'd long pursued it, I was, of course *happy*, and *covetous* of it.

I asked myself if I was wrong to covet it. And thought about it long, and, I hope, truthfully, and saw in myself several things in, I think, no particular order. (*Pause*)

That I *would* pursue it. That I *desired* it, that I was not pure of longing for security, and that that, perhaps, was not reprehensible in me. That I had duties *beyond* the school, and that my duty to my home, for instance, was, or should be, if it were not, of an equal weight. That tenure, and security, and yes, and *comfort,* were not, of themselves, to be scorned; and were even worthy of honorable pursuit. And that it was given me. Here, in this place, which I enjoy, and in which I find comfort, to assure myself of—as far as it rests in The Material—a continuation of that joy and comfort. In exchange for what? Teaching. Which I love.

What was the price of this security? To obtain *tenure.* Which tenure the committee is in the process of granting me. And on the basis of which I contracted to purchase a house. Now, as you don't have your own family, at this point, you may not know what that means. But to me it is important. A home. A Good Home. To raise my family. Now: The Tenure Committee will meet. This is the process, and a *good* process. Under which the school has functioned for quite a long time. They will meet, and hear your complaint—which you have the right to make; and they will dismiss it. They will *dismiss* your complaint; and, in the intervening period, I will lose my house. I will not be able to close on my house. I will lose my *deposit,* and the home I'd picked out for my wife and son will go by the boards. Now: I see I have angered you. I understand your anger at teachers. I was angry with mine. I felt hurt and humiliated by them. Which is one of the reasons that I went into education.

CAROL: What do you want of me?

JOHN: (*Pause*) I was hurt. When I received the report. Of the tenure committee. I was shocked. And I was hurt. No, I don't mean to subject you to my weak sensibilities. All right. Finally, I didn't understand. Then I thought: is it not always at those points at which we reckon ourselves unassailable that we are most vulnerable and . . . (*Pause*) Yes. All right. You find me pedantic. Yes. I am. By nature, by *birth,* by profession, I don't know . . . I'm always looking for a *paradigm* for . . .

CAROL: I don't know what a paradigm is.

JOHN: It's a model.

CAROL: Then why can't you use that word? (*Pause*)

JOHN: If it is important to you. Yes, all right. I was looking for a model. To continue: I feel that one point . . .

CAROL: I . . .

JOHN: One second . . . upon which I am unassailable is my unflinching concern for my students' dignity. I asked you here to . . . in the spirit of *investigation,* to ask you . . . to ask . . . (*Pause*) What have I done to you? (*Pause*) And, and, I suppose, how I can make amends. Can we not settle this now? It's pointless, really, and I want to know.

CAROL: What you can do to force me to retract?

JOHN: That is not what I meant at all.

CAROL: To bribe me, to convince me . . .

JOHN: . . . No.

CAROL: To retract . . .

JOHN: That is not what I meant at all. I think that you know it is not.

CAROL: That is not what I know. I *wish* I . . .

JOHN: I do not want to . . . you wish what?

CAROL: No, you said what amends can you make. To force me to retract.

JOHN: That is not what I said.

CAROL: I have my notes.

JOHN: Look. Look. The Stoics say . . .

CAROL: The Stoics?

JOHN: The Stoical Philosophers say if you remove the phrase "I have been injured," you have removed the injury. Now: Think: I know that you're upset. Just tell me. Literally. Literally: what wrong have I done you?

CAROL: Whatever you have done to me—to the extent that you've done it to *me,* do you know, rather than to me as a *student,* and, so, to the student body, is contained in my report. To the tenure committee.

JOHN: Well, all right. (*Pause*) Let's see. (*He reads.*) I find that I am sexist. That I am *elitist.* I'm not sure I know what that means, other than it's a derogatory word, meaning "bad." That I . . . That I insist on wasting time, in nonprescribed, in self-aggrandizing and theatrical *diversions* from the prescribed *text* . . . that these have taken both sexist and pornographic forms . . . here we find listed . . . (*Pause*) Here we find listed . . . instances ". . . closeted with a student" . . . "Told a rambling, sexually explicit story, in which the frequency and attitudes of fornication of the poor and rich are, it would seem, the central point . . . moved to *embrace* said student and . . . all part of a pattern . . ." (*Pause*)

(*He reads.*) That I used the phrase "The White Man's Burden" . . . that I told you how I'd asked you to my room because I quote like you. (*Pause*)

(*He reads.*) "He said he 'liked' me. That he 'liked being with me.' He'd let me write my examination paper over, if I could come back oftener to see him in his office." (*Pause*) (*To* CAROL:) It's *ludicrous*. Don't you know that? It's not *necessary*. It's going to *humiliate* you, and it's going to cost me my *house*, and . . .

CAROL: It's "*ludicrous* . . ."?

(JOHN *picks up the report and reads again.*)

JOHN: "He told me he had problems with his wife; and that he wanted to take off the artificial stricture of Teacher and Student. He put his arm around me . . ."

CAROL: Do you deny it? Can you deny it . . . ? Do you see? (*Pause*) Don't you see? You don't see, do you?

JOHN: I don't see . . .

CAROL: You think, you think you can deny that these things happened; or, if they *did*, if they *did*, that they meant what you *said* they meant. Don't you see? You drag me in here, you drag us, to listen to you "go on"; and "go on" about this, or that, or we don't "express" ourselves very well. We don't say what we mean. Don't we? Don't we? We *do* say what we mean. And you say that "I don't understand you . . .": Then *you* . . . (*Points.*)

JOHN: "Consult the Report"?

CAROL: . . . that's right.

JOHN: You see. You see. Can't you . . . . You see what I'm saying? Can't you tell me in your own words?

CAROL: Those are my own words. (*Pause*)

JOHN: (*He reads.*) "He told me that if I would stay alone with him in his office, he would change my grade to an A." (*To* CAROL:) What have I done to you? Oh. My God, are you so hurt?

CAROL: What I "feel" is irrelevant. (*Pause*)

JOHN: Do you know that I tried to help you?

CAROL: What I know I have reported.

JOHN: I would like to help you now. I would. Before this escalates.

CAROL (*simultaneously with* "escalates"): You see. I don't think that I need your help. I don't think I need anything you have.

JOHN: I feel . . .

CAROL: I don't *care* what you feel. Do you see? DO YOU SEE? You can't *do* that anymore. You. Do. Not. Have. The. Power. Did you misuse it? *Someone* did. Are you part of that group? *Yes. Yes.* You Are. You've *done* these things. And to say, and to say, "Oh. Let me help you with your problem . . ."

JOHN: Yes. I understand. I understand. You're *hurt*. You're *angry*. Yes. I think your *anger* is *betraying* you. Down a path which helps no one.

CAROL: I don't *care* what you think.

JOHN: You don't? (*Pause*) But you talk of *rights*. Don't you see? *I* have rights too. Do you see? I have a *house* . . . part of the *real* world; and The Tenure Committee, Good Men and True . . .

CAROL: . . . Professor . . .

JOHN: . . . Please: *Also* part of that world: you understand? This is my *life*. I'm not a *bogeyman*. I don't "stand" for something, I . . .

CAROL: . . . Professor . . .

JOHN: . . . I . . .

CAROL: Professor. I came here as a *favor*. At your personal request. Perhaps I should not have done so.

But I did. On my behalf, and on behalf of my group. And you speak of the tenure committee, one of whose members is a woman, as you know. And though you might call it Good Fun, or An Historical Phrase, or An Oversight, or, All of the Above, to refer to the committee as Good Men and True, it is a demeaning remark. It is a sexist remark, and to overlook it is to countenance continuation of that method of thought. It's a remark . . .

JOHN: OH COME ON. Come on. . . . Sufficient to deprive a family of . . .

CAROL: Sufficient? Sufficient? Sufficient? Yes. It is a *fact* . . . and that story, which I quote, is *vile* and *classist*, and *manipulative* and *pornographic*. It . . .

JOHN: . . . it's pornographic . . . ?

CAROL: What gives you the *right*. Yes. To speak to a *woman* in your private . . . Yes. Yes. I'm sorry. I'm sorry. You feel yourself empowered . . . you say so yourself. To *strut*. To *posture*. To "perform." To "Call me in here . . ." Eh? You say that higher education is a joke. And treat it as such, you *treat* it as such. And *confess* to a taste to play the *Patriarch* in your class. To grant *this*. To deny *that*. To embrace your students.

JOHN: How can you assert. How can you stand there and . . .

CAROL: How can you *deny* it. You did it to me. *Here*.
     You *did* . . . . You *confess*. You love the Power.
     To *deviate*. To *invent*, to transgress . . . to *trans-*
     gress whatever norms have been established for
     us. And you think it's charming to "question" in
     yourself this taste to mock and destroy. But you
     should question it. Professor. And you pick those
     things which you feel *advance* you: publication,
     tenure, and the steps to get them you call "harm-
     less rituals." And you perform those steps. Al-
     though you say it is hypocrisy. But to the
     aspirations of your students. Of *hardworking stu-*
     dents, who come here, who *slave* to come here—
     you have no idea what it cost me to come to this
     school—you *mock* us. You call education "haz-
     ing," and from your so-protected, so-elitist seat
     you hold our confusion as a *joke*, and our hopes
     and efforts with it. Then you sit there and say
     "what have I done?" And ask me to understand
     that *you* have aspirations too. But I tell you. I tell
     you. That you are vile. And that you are ex-
     ploitative. And if you possess one ounce of that
     inner honesty you describe in your book, you
     can look in yourself and see those things that I
     see. And you can find revulsion equal to my
     own. Good day. (*She prepares to leave the room.*)

JOHN: Wait a second, will you, just one moment.
     (*Pause*) Nice day today.

CAROL: What?

JOHN: You said "Good day." I think that it is a nice day today.

CAROL: *Is* it?

JOHN: Yes, I think it is.

CAROL: And why is that important?

JOHN: Because it is the essence of all human communication. I say something conventional, you respond, and the information we exchange is not about the "weather," but that we both agree to converse. In effect, we agree that we are both human. (*Pause*)

I'm not a . . . "exploiter," and you're not a . . . "deranged," what? *Revolutionary* . . . that we may, that we may have . . . positions, and that we may have . . . desires, which are in *conflict*, but that we're just human. (*Pause*) That means that sometimes we're *imperfect*. (*Pause*) Often we're in conflict . . . (*Pause*) *Much* of what we do, you're right, in the name of "principles" is *self-serving* . . . much of what we do is *conventional*. (*Pause*) You're right. (*Pause*) You said you came in the class because you wanted to learn about *education*. I don't know that I can teach you about education. But I know that I can tell you what I *think* about education, and then *you* decide. And you don't have to fight with me. *I'm* not the subject. (*Pause*) And where I'm *wrong* . . . perhaps it's not your job to "fix" me. I don't want to fix *you*. I would like to tell you what I *think*, because that *is* my job, conventional as it is, and flawed as I may be. And then, if you can show me some better *form*, then we can proceed from there. But, just like "nice day, isn't it . . . ?" I don't think we can proceed until we accept that each of us is human. (*Pause*) And we still can have difficulties. We *will* have them . . . that's all right too. (*Pause*) Now:

CAROL: . . . wait . . .

JOHN: Yes. I want to hear it.

CAROL: . . . the . . .

JOHN: Yes. Tell me frankly.

CAROL: . . . my position . . .

JOHN: I want to hear it. In your own words. What you want. And what you feel.

CAROL: . . . I . . .

JOHN: . . . yes . . .

CAROL: My Group.

JOHN: Your "Group" . . . ? (*Pause*)

CAROL: The people I've been talking to . . .

JOHN: There's no shame in that. Everybody needs advisers. Everyone needs to expose themselves. To various points of view. It's not wrong. It's essential. Good. Good. Now: You and I . . . (*The phone rings.*)
You and I . . .
(*He hesitates for a moment, and then picks it up.*) (*Into phone*) Hello. (*Pause*) Um . . . no, I know they do. (*Pause*) I know she does. Tell her that I . . . can I call you back? . . . Then tell her that I think it's going to be fine. (*Pause*) Tell her just, just hold on, I'll . . . can I get back to you? . . . Well . . . no, no, no, we're *taking* the house . . . we're . . . no, no, nn . . . no, she will nnn, it's not a *question* of refunding the dep . . . no . . . it's not a *question* of the deposit . . . will you call Jerry? Babe, baby, will you just call Jerry? Tell him, nnn . . . tell him they, well, they're to keep the deposit, because the deal, be . . . because the deal is going to go *through* . . . because I know . . . be . . . will you please? Just *trust* me. Be . . . well, I'm dealing with the complaint. Yes. Right *Now.* Which is why I . . . yes, no, no, it's really, I can't *talk* about it now. Call Jerry, and I can't talk now. Ff . . . fine. Gg . . . good-bye. (*Hangs up.*) (*Pause*) I'm sorry we were interrupted.

CAROL: No . . .

JOHN: I . . . I was saying:

CAROL: You said that we should agree to talk about my complaint.

JOHN: That's correct.

CAROL: But we *are* talking about it.

JOHN: Well, that's correct too. You see? This is the *gist* of education.

CAROL: No, no. I mean, we're talking about it at the Tenure Committee Hearing. (*Pause*)

JOHN: Yes, but I'm saying: we can talk about it *now,* as easily as . . .

CAROL: No. I think that we should stick to the process . . .

JOHN: . . . wait a . . .

CAROL: . . . the "conventional" process. As you said. (*She gets up.*) And you're right, I'm sorry if I was, um, if I was "discourteous" to you. You're right.

JOHN: Wait, wait a . . .

CAROL: I really should go.

JOHN: Now, look, granted. I have an interest. In the status quo. All right? Everyone does. But what I'm saying is that the *committee* . . .

CAROL: Professor, you're right. Just don't impinge on me. We'll take our differences, and . . .

JOHN: You're going to make a . . . look, look, look, you're going to . . .

CAROL: I shouldn't have come here. They told me . . .

JOHN: One moment. No. No. There are *norms,* here, and there's no reason. Look: I'm trying to *save* you . . .

CAROL: No one *asked* you to . . . you're trying to save *me?* Do me the courtesy to . . .

JOHN: I *am* doing you the courtesy. I'm talking *straight* to you. We can settle this *now.* And I want you to sit *down* and . . .

CAROL: You must excuse me . . . (*She starts to leave the room.*)

JOHN: Sit down, it seems we each have a . . . . Wait one moment. Wait one moment . . . just do me the courtesy to . . .
(*He restrains her from leaving.*)

CAROL: LET ME GO.

JOHN: I have no desire to *hold* you, I just want to *talk* to you . . .

CAROL: LET ME GO. LET ME GO. WOULD SOMEBODY *HELP* ME? WOULD SOME-BODY *HELP* ME PLEASE . . . ?

THREE

□□□

(At rise, CAROL *and* JOHN *are seated.)*

JOHN: I have asked you here. *(Pause)* I have asked you
here against, against my . . .

CAROL: I was most surprised you asked me.

JOHN: . . . against my better *judgment,* against . . .

CAROL: I was most surprised . . .

JOHN: . . . against the . . . yes. I'm sure.

CAROL: . . . If you would like me to leave, I'll leave.
I'll go right now . . . *(She rises.)*

JOHN: Let us begin *correctly,* may we? I feel . . .

CAROL: That is what I wished to do. That's why I
came here, but now . . .

JOHN: . . . I feel . . .

CAROL: But now perhaps you'd like me to leave . . .

JOHN: I don't want you to leave. I asked you to come . . .

CAROL: I didn't have to come here.

JOHN: No. (*Pause*) Thank you.

CAROL: All right. (*Pause*) (*She sits down.*)

JOHN: Although I feel that it *profits*, it would *profit* you something, to . . .

CAROL: . . . what I . . .

JOHN: If you would hear me out, if you would hear me out.

CAROL: I came here to, the court officers told me not to come.

JOHN: . . . the "court" officers . . . ?

CAROL: I was shocked that you asked.

JOHN: . . . wait . . .

CAROL: Yes. But I did *not* come here to hear what it "profits" me.

JOHN: The "court" officers . . .

CAROL: . . . no, no, perhaps I should leave . . . (*She gets up*.)

JOHN: Wait.

CAROL: No. I shouldn't have . . .

JOHN: . . . wait. Wait. Wait a moment.

CAROL: Yes? What is it you want? (*Pause*) What is it you want?

JOHN: I'd like you to stay.

CAROL: You want me to stay.

JOHN: Yes.

CAROL: You do.

JOHN: Yes. (*Pause*) Yes. I would like to have you hear me out. If you would. (*Pause*) Would you please? If you would do that I would be in your debt. (*Pause*) (*She sits*.) Thank You. (*Pause*)

CAROL: What is it you wish to tell me?

JOHN: All right. I cannot . . . (*Pause*) I cannot help but feel you are owed an apology. (*Pause*) (*Of papers in his hands*) I have read. (*Pause*) And reread these accusations.

CAROL: What "accusations"?

JOHN: The, the tenure comm . . . what other accusations . . . ?

CAROL: The tenure committee . . . ?

JOHN: Yes.

CAROL: Excuse me, but those are not accusations. They have been *proved*. They are facts.

JOHN: . . . I . . .

CAROL: No. Those are not "accusations."

JOHN: . . . those?

CAROL: . . . the committee (*The phone starts to ring.*) the committee has . . .

JOHN: . . . All right . . .

CAROL: . . . those are not accusations. The Tenure Committee.

JOHN: ALL RIGHT. ALL RIGHT. ALL RIGHT. (*He picks up the phone.*) Hello. Yes. No. I'm here. Tell Mister . . . No, I can't talk to him now . . . I'm sure he has, but I'm fff . . . I know . . . No, I have no time t . . . tell Mister . . . tell Mist . . . tell Jerry that I'm *fine* and that I'll call

him right aw . . . (*Pause*) My wife . . . Yes. I'm
sure she has. Yes, thank you. Yes, I'll call her
too. I cannot talk to you now. (*He hangs up.*)
(*Pause*) All right. It was good of you to come.
Thank you. I have studied. I have spent some
time studying the indictment.

CAROL: You will have to explain that word to me.

JOHN: An "indictment" . . .

CAROL: Yes.

JOHN: Is a "bill of particulars." A . . .

CAROL: All right. Yes.

JOHN: In which is alleged . . .

CAROL: No. I cannot allow that. I cannot allow that.
Nothing is alleged. Everything is proved . . .

JOHN: Please, wait a sec . . .

CAROL: I cannot *come* to allow . . .

JOHN: If I may . . . If I may, from whatever you feel
is "established," by . . .

CAROL: The issue here is not what I "feel." It is not
my "feelings," but the feelings of women. And
men. Your superiors, who've been "polled," do

you see? To whom *evidence* has been presented, who have *ruled*, do you see? Who have weighed the testimony and the evidence, and have *ruled*, do you see? That you are *negligent*. That you are *guilty*, that you are found *wanting*, and in *error*; and are *not*, for the reasons so-told, to be given tenure. That you are to be disciplined. For facts. For *facts*. Not "alleged," what is the word? But *proved*. Do you see? *By your own actions*.

That is what the tenure committee has said. That is what my lawyer said. For what you did in class. For what you did *in this office*.

JOHN: They're going to discharge me.

CAROL: As full well they should. You don't understand? You're angry? What has *led* you to this place? Not your sex. Not your race. Not your class. YOUR OWN ACTIONS. And you're *angry*. You *ask* me here. What *do* you want? You want to "charm" me. You want to "convince" me. You want me to recant. I will *not* recant. Why should I . . . ? What I say is right. You tell me, you are going to tell me that you have a wife and child. You are going to say that you have a career and that you've worked for twenty years for this. Do you know what you've *worked* for? *Power*. For *power*. Do you understand? And you sit there, and you tell me *stories*. About your *house*, about all the private *schools*, and about *privilege*, and how you are entitled. To *buy*, to *spend*, to *mock*, to *summon*. All your stories. All your silly weak *guilt*, it's all about *privilege;* and you won't know it. Don't you see? You worked twenty years for the right to *insult* me. And you feel entitled to be *paid* for it. Your Home. Your Wife . . . Your sweet "deposit" on your house . . .

JOHN: Don't you have feelings?

CAROL: That's my point. You see? Don't you have feelings? Your final argument. What is it that has no feelings. *Animals.* I don't take your side, you question if I'm Human.

JOHN: Don't you have feelings?

CAROL: I have a responsibility. I . . .

JOHN: . . . to . . . ?

CAROL: To? This institution. To the *students*. To my *group*.

JOHN: . . . your "group." . . .

CAROL: Because I speak, yes, not for myself. But for the group; for those who suffer what I suffer. On behalf of whom, even if I, were, inclined, to what, forgive? Forget? What? Overlook your . . .

JOHN: . . . my behavior?

CAROL: . . . it would be wrong.

JOHN: Even if you were inclined to "forgive" me.

CAROL: It would be wrong.

JOHN: And what would transpire.

CAROL: Transpire?

JOHN: Yes.

CAROL: "Happen?"

JOHN: Yes.

CAROL: Then *say* it. For Christ's sake. Who the *hell* do
you think that you are? You want a post. You
want unlimited power. To do and to say what
you want. As it pleases you—Testing, Questioning, Flirting . . .

JOHN: I never . . .

CAROL: Excuse me, one moment, will you?
(*She reads from her notes.*)
    The twelfth: "Have a good day, dear."
    The fifteenth: "Now, don't *you* look
fetching . . ."
    April seventeenth: "If you girls would come
over here . . ." I saw you. I saw you, Professor.
For two semesters sit there, stand there and ex-

ploit our, as you thought, "paternal preroga-
tive," and what is that but rape; I swear to God.
You asked me in here to explain something to
me, as a child, that I did not understand. But I
came to explain something to you. You Are Not
God. You ask me why I came? I came here to
instruct you.

(She produces his book.)

And your book? You think you're going to
show me some "light"? You *"maverick."* Outside of tradition. No, no, *(She reads from the book's
liner notes.)* *"of* that fine tradition of *inquiry.* Of
Polite *skepticism"* . . . and you say you believe in
free intellectual discourse. YOU BELIEVE IN
NOTHING. YOU BELIEVE IN NOTHING
AT ALL.

JOHN: I believe in freedom of thought.

CAROL: Isn't that fine. *Do* you?

JOHN: Yes. I do.

CAROL: Then why do you question, for one moment,
the committee's decision refusing your tenure?
Why do you question your suspension? You
believe in what *you call* freedom of thought.
Then, fine. *You* believe in freedom-of-thought
and a home, and, *and* prerogatives for your kid,
and tenure. And I'm going to tell you. You
believe *not* in "freedom of thought," but in an
elitist, in, in a protected hierarchy which rewards

you. And for whom you are the clown. And you mock and exploit the system which pays your rent. You're wrong. I'm not wrong. You're wrong. You think that I'm full of hatred. I know what you think I am.

JOHN: Do you?

CAROL: You think I'm a, of course I do. You think I am a frightened, repressed, confused, I don't know, abandoned young thing of some doubtful sexuality, who wants, power and revenge. (*Pause*) *Don't* you? (*Pause*)

JOHN: Yes. I do. (*Pause*)

CAROL: Isn't that better? And I feel that that is the first moment which you've treated me with respect. For you told me the truth. (*Pause*) I did not come here, as you are assured, to gloat. Why would I want to gloat? I've profited nothing from your, your, as you say, your "misfortune." I came here, as you did me the honor to *ask* me here, I came here to *tell* you something.

(*Pause*) That I think . . . that I think you've been wrong. That I think you've been terribly wrong. Do you hate me now? (*Pause*)

JOHN: Yes.

CAROL: Why do you hate me? Because you think me wrong? No. Because I have, you think, *power* over you. Listen to me. Listen to me, Professor. (*Pause*) It is the power that you hate. So deeply that, that any atmosphere of free discussion is impossible. It's not "unlikely." It's *impossible*. Isn't it?

JOHN: Yes.

CAROL: *Isn't* it . . . ?

JOHN: Yes. I suppose.

CAROL: Now. The thing which you find so cruel is the selfsame process of selection I, and my group, go through *every day of our lives*. In admittance to school. In our tests, in our class rankings. . . . Is it unfair? I can't tell you. But, if it is fair. Or even if it is "unfortunate but necessary" for us, then, by God, so must it be for you. (*Pause*) You write of your "responsibility to the young." Treat us with respect, and that will *show* you your responsibility. You write that education is just hazing. (*Pause*) But we worked to get to this school. (*Pause*) And some of us. (*Pause*) Overcame prejudices. Economic, sexual, you cannot begin to imagine. And endured humiliations I *pray* that you and those you love never will encounter. (*Pause*) To gain admittance here. To pursue that same dream of security *you* pursue. We, who, who are, at any moment, in danger of being deprived of it. By . . .

JOHN: . . . by . . . ?

CAROL: By the administration. By the teachers. By *you*. By, say, one low grade, that keeps us out of graduate school; by one, say, one capricious or inventive answer on our parts, which, perhaps, you don't find amusing. Now you *know,* do you see? What it is to be subject to that power. (*Pause*)

JOHN: I don't understand. (*Pause*)

CAROL: My charges are not trivial. You see that in the haste, I think, with which they were accepted. A *joke* you have told, with a sexist tinge. The language you use, a verbal or physical caress, yes, yes, I know, you say that it is meaningless. I understand. I differ from you. To lay a hand on someone's shoulder.

JOHN: It was devoid of sexual content.

CAROL: I say it was not. I SAY IT WAS NOT. Don't you begin to *see* . . . ? Don't you begin to understand? IT'S NOT FOR YOU TO SAY.

JOHN: I take your point, and I see there is much good in what you refer to.

CAROL: . . . do you think so . . . ?

JOHN: . . . but, and this is not to say that I cannot change, in those things in which I am deficient . . . But, the . . .

CAROL: Do you hold yourself harmless from the charge of sexual exploitativeness . . . ? (*Pause*)

JOHN: Well, I . . . I . . . I . . . You know I, as I said. I . . . think I am not too old to *learn,* and I *can* learn, I . . .

CAROL: Do you hold yourself innocent of the charge of . . .

JOHN: . . . wait, wait, wait . . . All right, let's go back to . . .

CAROL: YOU FOOL. Who do you think I am? To come here and be taken in by a *smile.* You little yapping fool. You think I want "revenge." I don't want revenge. I WANT UNDER-STANDING.

JOHN: . . . *do* you?

CAROL: I do. (*Pause*)

JOHN: What's the use. It's over.

CAROL: Is it? What is?

JOHN: My job.

CAROL: Oh. Your job. That's what you want to talk about. (*Pause*) (*She starts to leave the room. She steps and turns back to him.*) All right. (*Pause*) What if it were possible that my Group withdraws its complaint. (*Pause*)

JOHN: What?

CAROL: That's right. (*Pause*)

JOHN: Why.

CAROL: Well, let's say as an act of friendship.

JOHN: An act of friendship.

CAROL: Yes. (*Pause*)

JOHN: In exchange for what.

CAROL: Yes. But I don't think, "exchange." Not "in exchange." For what do we derive from it? (*Pause*)

JOHN: "Derive."

CAROL: Yes.

JOHN: (*Pause*) Nothing. (*Pause*)

CAROL: That's right. We derive nothing. (*Pause*) Do you see that?

JOHN: Yes.

CAROL: That is a little word, Professor. "Yes." "I see that." But you will.

JOHN: And you might speak to the committee . . . ?

CAROL: To the committee?

JOHN: Yes.

CAROL: Well. Of course. That's on your mind. We might.

JOHN: "If" what?

CAROL: "Given" what. Perhaps. I think that that is more friendly.

JOHN: GIVEN WHAT?

CAROL: And, believe me, I understand your rage. It is not that I don't feel it. But I do not see that it is deserved, so I do not resent it . . . . All right. I have a list.

JOHN: . . . a list.

CAROL: Here is a list of books, which we . . .

JOHN: . . . a list of books . . . ?

CAROL: That's right. Which we find questionable.

JOHN: What?

CAROL: Is this so bizarre . . . ?

JOHN: I can't believe . . .

CAROL: It's not necessary you believe it.

JOHN: Academic freedom . . .

CAROL: Someone chooses the books. If you can choose them, others can. What are you, "God"?

JOHN: . . . no, no, the "dangerous." . . .

CAROL: You have an agenda, we have an agenda. I am not interested in your feelings or your motivation, but your actions. If you would like me to speak to the Tenure Committee, here is my list. You are a Free Person, you decide. (*Pause*)

JOHN: Give me the list. (*She does so. He reads.*)

CAROL: I think you'll find . . .

JOHN: I'm capable of reading it. Thank you.

CAROL: We have a number of *texts* we need re . . .

JOHN: I see that.

CAROL: We're amenable to . . .

JOHN: Aha. Well, let me look over the . . . (*He reads.*)

CAROL: I think that . . .

JOHN: LOOK. I'm reading your demands. All right?! (*He reads*) (*Pause*) You want to ban my book?

CAROL: We do not . . .

JOHN (*Of list*): It says here . . .

CAROL: . . . We want it removed from inclusion as a representative example of the university.

JOHN: Get out of here.

CAROL: If you put aside the issues of personalities.

JOHN: Get the fuck out of my office.

CAROL: No, I think I would reconsider.

JOHN: . . . you think you can.

CAROL: We can and we *will*. Do you want our support? That is the only quest . . .

JOHN: . . . to ban my *book* . . . ?

CAROL: . . . that is correct . . .

JOHN: . . . this . . . this is a *university* . . . we . . .

CAROL: . . . and we have a statement . . . which we need you to . . . (*She hands him a sheet of paper.*)

JOHN: No, no. It's out of the question. I'm sorry. I don't know what I was thinking of. I want to tell you something. I'm a teacher. I am a teacher. Eh? It's my *name* on the door, and *I* teach the class, and that's what I do. I've got a book with my name on it. And my son will *see* that *book* someday. And I have a respon . . . No, I'm sorry I have a *responsibility* . . . to *myself,* to my *son,* to my *profession.* . . . I haven't been *home* for two days, do you know that? Thinking this out.

CAROL: . . . you haven't?

JOHN: I've been, no. If it's of interest to you. I've been in a *hotel. Thinking.* (*The phone starts ringing.*) *Thinking* . . .

CAROL: . . . you haven't been home?

JOHN: . . . *thinking,* do you see.

CAROL: Oh.

JOHN: And, and, I owe you a debt, I see that now. (*Pause*) You're *dangerous,* you're *wrong* and it's my *job* . . . to say no to you. That's my job. You are absolutely right. You want to ban my book? Go to *hell,* and they can do whatever they want to me.

CAROL: . . . you haven't been home in two days . . .

JOHN: I think I told you that.

CAROL: . . . you'd better get that phone. (*Pause*) I think that you should pick up the phone. (*Pause*)

(JOHN *picks up the phone.*)

JOHN (*on phone*): Yes. (*Pause*) Yes. Wh . . . I. I. I had to be away. All ri . . . did they wor . . . did they worry ab . . . No. I'm all right, now, Jerry. I'm f . . . I got a little turned *around*, but I'm *sitting* here and . . . I've got it figured out. I'm fine. I'm fine don't worry about me. I got a little bit mixed up. But I am not sure that it's not a blessing. It cost me my job? Fine. Then the job was not worth having. Tell Grace that I'm coming home and everything is fff . . . (*Pause*) What? (*Pause*) *What?* (*Pause*) What do you *mean?* WHAT? Jerry . . . Jerry. They . . . Who, who, what can they do . . . ? (*Pause*) NO. (*Pause*) NO. They can't do th . . . What do you mean? (*Pause*) But how . . . (*Pause*) She's, she's, she's *here* with me. To . . . Jerry. I don't underst . . . (*Pause*) (*He hangs up.*) (*To* CAROL:) What does this mean?

CAROL: I thought you knew.

JOHN: What. (*Pause*) What does it mean. (*Pause*)

CAROL: You tried to rape me. (*Pause*) According to the law. (*Pause*)

JOHN: . . . what . . . ?

CAROL: You tried to rape me. I was leaving this office, you "pressed" yourself into me. You "pressed" your body into me.

JOHN: . . . I . . .

CAROL: My Group has told your lawyer that we may pursue criminal charges.

JOHN: . . . no . . .

CAROL: . . . under the statute. I am told. It was battery.

JOHN: . . . no . . .

CAROL: Yes. And attempted rape. That's right. (*Pause*)

JOHN: I think that you should go.

CAROL: Of course. I thought you knew.

JOHN: I have to talk to my lawyer.

CAROL: Yes. Perhaps you should.
(*The phone rings again.*) (*Pause*)

JOHN: (*Picks up phone. Into phone:*) Hello? I . . . Hello . . . ? I . . . Yes, he just called. No . . . I. I can't talk to you now, Baby. (*To* CAROL:) Get out.

CAROL: . . . your wife . . . ?

JOHN: . . . who it is is no concern of yours. Get out.
(*To phone:*) No, no, it's going to be all right. I.
I can't talk now, Baby. (*To* CAROL:) Get out of
here.

CAROL: I'm going.

JOHN: Good.

CAROL (*exiting*): . . . and don't call your wife "baby."

JOHN: What?

CAROL: Don't call your wife baby. You heard what I
said.

(CAROL *starts to leave the room.* JOHN *grabs her and begins
to beat her.*)

JOHN: You vicious little bitch. You think you can
come in here with your political correctness and
destroy my life?

(*He knocks her to the floor.*)

After how I treated you . . . ? You should be
. . . *Rape you* . . . ? Are you kidding me . . . ?

(*He picks up a chair, raises it above his head, and
advances on her.*)

I wouldn't touch you with a ten-foot pole. You
little *cunt* . . .

(*She cowers on the floor below him. Pause. He looks down at her. He lowers the chair. He moves to his desk, and arranges the papers on it. Pause. He looks over at her.*)

. . . well . . .

(*Pause. She looks at him.*)

CAROL: Yes. That's right.

(*She looks away from him, and lowers her head. To herself:*) . . . yes. That's right.

END

Notes

2 *'easement'*: legal term for a right of way over someone's property.

realtor: estate agent.

the deposit: non-refundable sum paid by the prospective purchaser of a property to the vendor on exchange of contracts; typically ten per cent of the purchase price.

5 *obeisance*: archaic term for obedience or respect.

17 *verbiage*: excessive use of words, without much meaning; John is insisting that what he says is sincerely meant.

21 *stricture*: a tight bond or restriction, in this context the rules that separate teachers and students and define their relationships.

23 *tenure*: guaranteed permanent employment for a university teacher, giving greater income and job security than the short, renewable contracts under which most teachers in higher education (including John) are employed. Tenure is therefore something of a holy grail for academics and difficult to achieve.

27 *hazing*: John defines hazing in higher education as the 'ritualized annoyance' of students by their teachers, but in America 'hazing' is commonly used to refer to the cruel horseplay among American undergraduates, particularly those trying to gain admittance to fraternity (male) and sorority (female) houses. Senior members subject applicants to initiation rituals (beatings, enforced consumption of huge quantities of alcohol) that in several notorious cases have led to serious or fatal injuries. John's use of the term suggests, therefore, that the institutionalised bullying of students by teachers bears comparison with the illicit bullying of undergraduates by their peers. By late 2003, student hazing was of such concern that campus initiation ceremonies had been outlawed in more than forty US states.

33 *the School Tax*: tax levied to support public (i.e. state) education. John asks if the law that obliges him to pay the school tax also obliges him to send his son to a public (state) school funded by that tax. Doing so would be 'at the expense' of his interest in his son's future development, which he feels would be better served by sending him to private school. Why, he asks, must I pay for the education of other people's children as well as my own?

34 *The White Man's Burden*: this term originated during nineteenth-century European imperialism and refers to the assumed obligation of the whites (particularly the British) in each colonial territory to govern and educate the 'backward' black natives (see Rudyard Kipling's poem 'The White Man's Burden', 1899). Carol therefore views John's use of the phrase in his contemporary educational analogy as implicitly racist and presents it to the tenure committee as such.

I'm taking notes: the irony here is that Carol will not be using the notes for slavish regurgitation as John suspects but critically, thinking for herself – as John has encouraged – contributing to his undoing.

But if he does not learn: John typically uses the masculine pronoun which Carol switches to 'the child'. John obliviously carries on using the masculine.

43 *automaton*: machine which moves or person who acts in mechanical and monotonous fashion.

heterodoxy: the holding and/or teaching of opinions that deviate from the norm; deviation from orthodoxy (hence the description of John as a '*maverick*' on the jacket of his book, p.67).

47 *The Stoics*: school of Greek philosophers, founded by Zeno *c.* 300 BC, whose austere approach to life gave rise to the proverbial use of 'stoical', meaning indifference to pleasure or pain.

51 *Patriarch*: the male ruler of a family or community.

66 *the twelfth*: it turns out that Carol has been taking notes on John's behaviour from before the events of Act One, with the intention of making a complaint.

semesters: a college half-year. Many American universities divide the academic year into autumn and spring semesters, typically running from September to December and January to May, rather than autumn, winter and summer terms as in the UK.

67 *liner notes*: copy on the cover of a book, publisher's blurb and/or review quotes.

hierarchy: a governing body structured in ascending ranks.

70 *graduate school*: in America some form of second degree (e.g. a Master's in Business Administration, or MBA), obtained at graduate school, is a more common requirement for students hoping to obtain well-paid jobs than in the UK; hence Carol's concern that 'one low grade, that keeps us out of graduate school' can derail her and her peers' well-laid plans to get on in the world.

78 *battery*: legal term for an unlawful attack on another person by beating. Crucially, the technical definition may include 'the least touching of another's person or clothes in a menacing manner' (*Shorter Oxford English Dictionary*). This latter part of the definition makes 'battery' a credible charge to be levied against John for his forcible restraint of Carol at the end of Act Two; certainly more credible than attempted rape. During rehearsals for *Oleanna*'s Cambridge production, Mamet consulted Harvard law professor Alan Dershowitz, who offered advice on the legality of Carol's allegations and John's defence.

Questions for Further Study

1 David Mamet: 'I think they [Carol and John] are both absolutely wrong and absolutely both right.' To what extent are Carol and John responsible for what happens in the play? Who or what else may be held responsible and why?

2 What does *Oleanna* reveal of the goals, politics and methodology of higher education in the United States in the 1990s?

3 Using specific examples from the text, discuss how and why language becomes such a divisive barrier between John and Carol.

4 What do we know about John's and Carol's lives outside his study, and what impact do their respective family backgrounds have on their behaviour in the play?

5 Mamet believes that we are all bound by 'our lack of self-knowledge'. What do Carol and John learn about themselves during the course of the play? Have they changed as people by the end of Act Three and, if so, how?

6 'This is a play about power' (John Peter, *Sunday Times*). What different kinds of power are exercised by the on- and off-stage characters in *Oleanna*? Is this power used responsibly or abused?

7 Imagine that you are directing *Oleanna* for the theatre. How would you use Mamet's stage directions? How and when would you alter the respective positions of the two actors to underline the shifts in John and Carol's relationship? Give examples.

8 To cast your production of *Oleanna*, draw up a shortlist of five British or American actors and five British or American actresses to play John and Carol. With each name, refer to the actor's previous appearances on stage and/or screen to explain why you think they would be appropriate casting.

9 Look closely at pages 47–9, from 'Well, all right' (John) to 'What I "feel" is irrelevant' (Carol). In this quoted evidence

to the tenure committee, Carol refers to a number of comments made by John in Act One. Identifying them, discuss how John's language is open to subjective interpretation.

10 'It was certainly never a conscious decision on our part to play the sexual tension between them, but it's there in the text – something coming from her as much as him' (David Suchet on playing John). What evidence, whether implicit or explicit, is there in the text that John might be sexually interested in Carol, and vice versa?

11 Look closely at John's telephone conversations. How does Mamet use these to convey plot developments? What do John's telephone responses to his wife, Jerry and the realtor tells us and Carol about his character?

12 How does Carol's use of language change between Acts One, Two and Three? With examples, show how Mamet varies her vocabulary and the length of her speeches in each act to illustrate changes in her behaviour and personality.

13 Look at pages 43–5 (from the beginning of John's speech until 'Which is one of the reasons that I went into education'). How representative is this speech of John's strengths and weaknesses as a teacher in the play as a whole?

14 At various points in the play both John and Carol say 'I don't understand'. What is the meaning of 'understanding' in *Oleanna*? With examples, discuss this in relation to educational concepts and jargon, implicit and explicit intentions, and sympathy for another person's hopes, anxieties or failings.

15 Look at pages 66–70, from 'Excuse me, one moment, will you?' (Carol) to 'I don't understand' (John). To what extent do you believe this is an artificial, politically correct interpretation of John's writing and teaching rather than Carol's subjective response?

16 'A crude piece of theatre with little drama and zero ambiguity, with the cards grossly stacked against the female character' (Sarah Dunant). How far do you agree with this description of *Oleanna*?

17 'Carol is just an inadequate student seeking revenge against

the clever' (Anne Karpf). How far do you agree with this description of Carol and her behaviour?

18 At the first American performance of *Oleanna*, members of the audience applauded John's assault on Carol and a woman stood up as the house lights rose and said 'Let's find those guys who clapped'. How and why do you think the play provokes such strong feelings?

19 Does *Oleanna* challenge audience preconceptions about class, education and sexual harassment or reinforce them?

20 What thematic, dramatic or linguistic characteristics does *Oleanna* share with Mamet's other work? Discuss in relation to at least one other play, screenplay or collection of non-fiction theatre writing.

21 Compare and contrast the presentation of political correctness and sexual harassment in *Oleanna* with one or more of the following novels: *Disgrace* by J.M. Coetzee, *Disclosure* by Michael Crichton, *The Human Stain* by Philip Roth.

DANIEL ROSENTHAL was born in London in 1971 and educated at University College School, London, and Pembroke College, Cambridge. He has written on theatre and film for *The Times*, *Independent*, *Observer* and *Independent on Sunday*. He is Editor of the annual *Variety International Film Guide* and the author of *Shakespeare on Screen* (2000). He has written the Commentary and Notes for the Methuen Student Edition of Patrick Marber's *Closer* and he is writing a major new history of the Royal National Theatre.

Bloomsbury Methuen Drama Student Editions

Jean Anouilh *Antigone* • John Arden *Serjeant Musgrave's Dance*
Alan Ayckbourn *Confusions* • Aphra Behn *The Rover* • Edward Bond
Lear • *Saved* • Bertolt Brecht *The Caucasian Chalk Circle* • *Fear and
Misery in the Third Reich* • *The Good Person of Szechwan* • *Life of Galileo* •
Mother Courage and her Children• *The Resistible Rise of Arturo Ui* • *The
Threepenny Opera* • Anton Chekhov *The Cherry Orchard* • *The Seagull* •
Three Sisters • *Uncle Vanya* • Caryl Churchill *Serious Money* • *Top Girls*
• Shelagh Delaney *A Taste of Honey* • Euripides Elektra • *Medea*•
Dario Fo *Accidental Death of an Anarchist* • Michael Frayn *Copenhagen*
• John Galsworthy *Strife* • Nikolai Gogol *The Government Inspector* •
Robert Holman *Across Oka* • Henrik Ibsen *A Doll's House* • *Ghosts*•
Hedda Gabler • Charlotte Keatley *My Mother Said I Never Should* •
Bernard Kops *Dreams of Anne Frank* • Federico García Lorca *Blood
Wedding* • *Doña Rosita the Spinster* (bilingual edition) •*The House of
Bernarda Alba* • (bilingual edition) • *Yerma* (bilingual edition) • David
Mamet *Glengarry Glen Ross* • *Oleanna* • Patrick Marber *Closer* • John
Marston *The Malcontent* • Martin McDonagh *The Lieutenant of Inishmore* •
Joe Orton *Loot* • Luigi Pirandello *Six Characters in Search of an Author*
• Mark Ravenhill *Shopping and F***ing* • Willy Russell *Blood Brothers*
• *Educating Rita* • Sophocles *Antigone* • *Oedipus the King* • Wole
Soyinka *Death and the King's Horseman* • Shelagh Stephenson *The
Memory of Water* • August Strindberg *Miss Julie* • J. M. Synge *The
Playboy of the Western World* • Theatre Workshop *Oh What a Lovely
War* Timberlake Wertenbaker *Our Country's Good* • Arnold Wesker
The Merchant • Oscar Wilde *The Importance of Being Earnest* •
Tennessee Williams *A Streetcar Named Desire* • *The Glass Menagerie*

Bloomsbury Methuen Drama Modern Plays

include work by

Edward Albee	Howard Korder
Jean Anouilh	Robert Lepage
John Arden	Doug Lucie
Margaretta D'Arcy	Martin McDonagh
Peter Barnes	John McGrath
Sebastian Barry	Terrence McNally
Brendan Behan	David Mamet
Dermot Bolger	Patrick Marber
Edward Bond	Arthur Miller
Bertolt Brecht	Mtwa, Ngema & Simon
Howard Brenton	Tom Murphy
Anthony Burgess	Phyllis Nagy
Simon Burke	Peter Nichols
Jim Cartwright	Sean O'Brien
Caryl Churchill	Joseph O'Connor
Complicite	Joe Orton
Noël Coward	Louise Page
Lucinda Coxon	Joe Penhall
Sarah Daniels	Luigi Pirandello
Nick Darke	Stephen Poliakoff
Nick Dear	Franca Rame
Shelagh Delaney	Mark Ravenhill
David Edgar	Philip Ridley
David Eldridge	Reginald Rose
Dario Fo	Willy Russell
Michael Frayn	Jean-Paul Sartre
John Godber	Sam Shepard
Paul Godfrey	Wole Soyinka
David Greig	Simon Stephens
John Guare	Shelagh Stephenson
Peter Handke	Peter Straughan
David Harrower	C. P. Taylor
Jonathan Harvey	Theatre Workshop
Iain Heggie	Sue Townsend
Declan Hughes	Judy Upton
Terry Johnson	Timberlake Wertenbaker
Sarah Kane	Roy Williams
Charlotte Keatley	Snoo Wilson
Barrie Keeffe	Victoria Wood

Bloomsbury Methuen Drama Contemporary Dramatists

include

John Arden (two volumes)
Arden & D'Arcy
Peter Barnes (three volumes)
Sebastian Barry
Dermot Bolger
Edward Bond (eight volumes)
Howard Brenton
  (two volumes)
Richard Cameron
Jim Cartwright
Caryl Churchill (two volumes)
Sarah Daniels (two volumes)
Nick Darke
David Edgar (three volumes)
David Eldridge
Ben Elton
Dario Fo (two volumes)
Michael Frayn (three volumes)
David Greig
John Godber (four volumes)
Paul Godfrey
John Guare
Lee Hall (two volumes)
Peter Handke
Jonathan Harvey
  (two volumes)
Declan Hughes
Terry Johnson (three volumes)
Sarah Kane
Barrie Keeffe
Bernard-Marie Koltès
  (two volumes)
Franz Xaver Kroetz
David Lan
Bryony Lavery
Deborah Levy
Doug Lucie

David Mamet (four volumes)
Martin McDonagh
Duncan McLean
Anthony Minghella
  (two volumes)
Tom Murphy (six volumes)
Phyllis Nagy
Anthony Neilsen (two volumes)
Philip Osment
Gary Owen
Louise Page
Stewart Parker (two volumes)
Joe Penhall (two volumes)
Stephen Poliakoff
  (three volumes)
David Rabe (two volumes)
Mark Ravenhill (two volumes)
Christina Reid
Philip Ridley
Willy Russell
Eric-Emmanuel Schmitt
Ntozake Shange
Sam Shepard (two volumes)
Wole Soyinka (two volumes)
Simon Stephens (two volumes)
Shelagh Stephenson
David Storey (three volumes)
Sue Townsend
Judy Upton
Michel Vinaver
  (two volumes)
Arnold Wesker (two volumes)
Michael Wilcox
Roy Williams (three volumes)
Snoo Wilson (two volumes)
David Wood (two volumes)
Victoria Wood

Bloomsbury Methuen Drama World Classics

include

Jean Anouilh (two volumes)
Brendan Behan
Aphra Behn
Bertolt Brecht (eight volumes)
Büchner
Bulgakov
Calderón
Čapek
Anton Chekhov
Noël Coward (eight volumes)
Feydeau (two volumes)
Eduardo De Filippo
Max Frisch
John Galsworthy
Gogol
Gorky (two volumes)
Harley Granville Barker
   (two volumes)
Victor Hugo
Henrik Ibsen (six volumes)
Jarry

Lorca (three volumes)
Marivaux
Mustapha Matura
David Mercer (two volumes)
Arthur Miller (six volumes)
Molière
Musset
Peter Nichols (two volumes)
Joe Orton
A. W. Pinero
Luigi Pirandello
Terence Rattigan
   (two volumes)
W. Somerset Maugham
   (two volumes)
August Strindberg
   (three volumes)
J. M. Synge
Ramón del Valle-Inclán
Frank Wedekind
Oscar Wilde

For a complete listing of Bloomsbury
Methuen Drama titles, visit:
www.bloomsbury.com/drama

Follow us on Twitter and keep up to date
with our news and publications
@MethuenDrama